ELSTREE 175

Celebrating 175 Years of Elstree School

ELSTREE 175

Celebrating 175 Years of Elstree School

Hugo Vickers

UNICORN

Published in 2023 by
Unicorn, an imprint of Unicorn Publishing Group
Charleston Studio
Meadow Business Centre
Lewes BN8 5RW
www.unicornpublishing.org

ISBN 978 1 911397 38 0
10 9 8 7 6 5 4 3 2 1

Design by newtonworks.uk
Printed in Malta by Gutenberg Press

CONTENTS

FOREWORD

James Sunley

Chairman of the Governors

To celebrate Elstree's 175th anniversary, we have produced a new history of the School which complements and adds a good deal of colour to the one written by Commander Ian Sanderson in 1979. I was fortunate enough to be at Elstree myself as a pupil in the early seventies when the School just topped 100 boys for the first time. Over the years my family has been closely involved with the welfare and development of the school. I now have the privilege of serving as Chairman of the Governors.

It has been great fun reading this lively account of school life over a period fast approaching 200 years. I am struck by how schools like Elstree have changed from being places of a certain severity into a modern environment, in which the young, entrusted to our care, are nurtured and prepared to go on to their senior schools and out into life. Elstree's stunning grounds will have enhanced the holistic learning experience and also the wealth of extra curricular activities pupils are so fortunate to play and learn. I can't help wondering what the early schoolmasters would have made of girls in the School, but their arrival has been a resounding success and made Elstree an even happier and livelier place than it was before.

We have been lucky in our author. Many school histories are written by retired headmasters, who look back nostalgically to their pasts, with a heavy emphasis on cricket scores and football matches long forgotten. Hugo Vickers is a well-known biographer. He did not go to Elstree himself, though his sons Arthur and George went through the School. So he knows it very well and at the same time has the objectivity of an outsider and is one well used to exploring archives. He has winkled out some wonderful stories.

I hope you will enjoy this book as much as I did.

Clarior ex Obscuro

SANDERSON FAMILY TREE

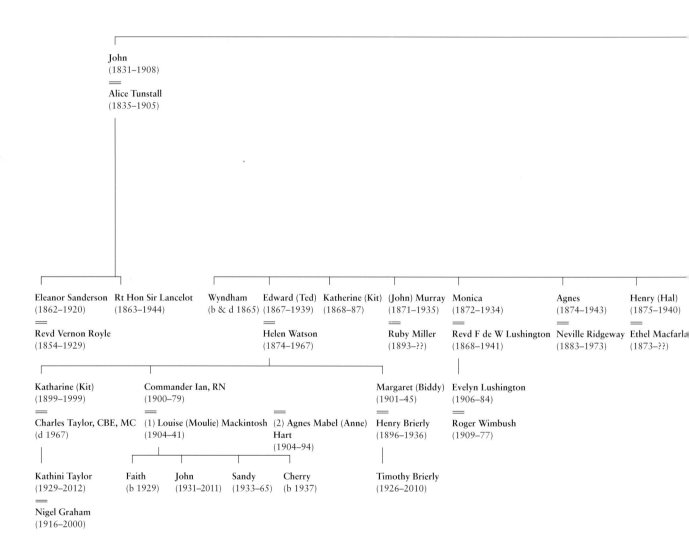

John
(1831–1908)
═══
Alice Tunstall
(1835–1905)

Eleanor Sanderson
(1862–1920)
═══
Revd Vernon Royle
(1854–1929)

Rt Hon Sir Lancelot
(1863–1944)

Wyndham
(b & d 1865)

Edward (Ted)
(1867–1939)
═══
Helen Watson
(1874–1967)

Katherine (Kit)
(1868–87)

(John) Murray
(1871–1935)
═══
Ruby Miller
(1893–??)

Monica
(1872–1934)
═══
Revd F de W Lushington
(1868–1941)

Agnes
(1874–1943)
═══
Neville Ridgeway
(1883–1973)

Henry (Hal)
(1875–1940)
═══
Ethel Macfarla
(1873–??)

Katharine (Kit)
(1899–1999)
═══
Charles Taylor, CBE, MC
(d 1967)

Commander Ian, RN
(1900–79)
═══
(1) Louise (Moulie) Mackintosh
(1904–41)
═══
(2) Agnes Mabel (Anne)
Hart
(1904–94)

Margaret (Biddy)
(1901–45)
═══
Henry Brierly
(1896–1936)

Evelyn Lushington
(1906–84)
═══
Roger Wimbush
(1909–77)

Kathini Taylor
(1929–2012)
═══
Nigel Graham
(1916–2000)

Faith
(b 1929)

John
(1931–2011)

Sandy
(1933–65)

Cherry
(b 1937)

Timothy Brierly
(1926–2010)

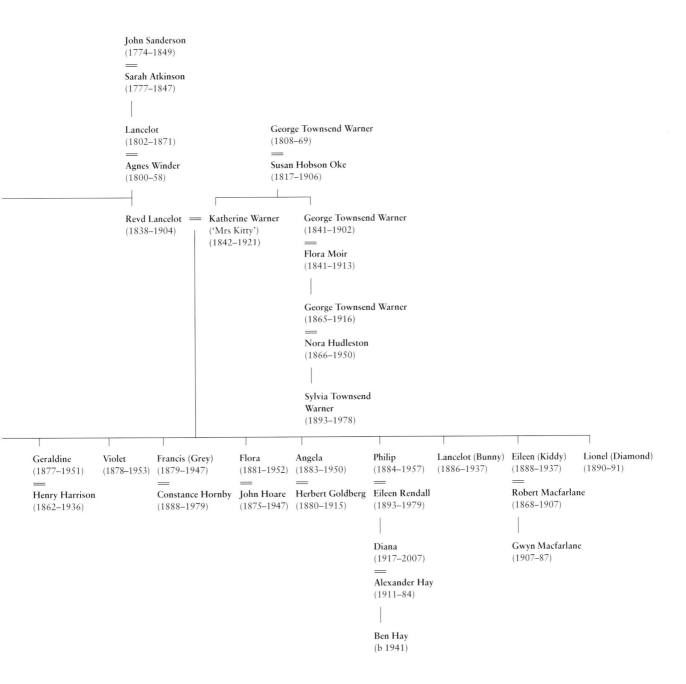

John Sanderson
(1774–1849)
=
Sarah Atkinson
(1777–1847)

Lancelot
(1802–1871)
=
Agnes Winder
(1800–58)

George Townsend Warner
(1808–69)
=
Susan Hobson Oke
(1817–1906)

Revd Lancelot
(1838–1904)
= Katherine Warner
('Mrs Kitty')
(1842–1921)

George Townsend Warner
(1841–1902)
=
Flora Moir
(1841–1913)

George Townsend Warner
(1865–1916)
=
Nora Hudleston
(1866–1950)

Sylvia Townsend
Warner
(1893–1978)

Geraldine
(1877–1951)
=
Henry Harrison
(1862–1936)

Violet
(1878–1953)

Francis (Grey)
(1879–1947)
=
Constance Hornby
(1888–1979)

Flora
(1881–1952)
=
John Hoare
(1875–1947)

Angela
(1883–1950)
=
Herbert Goldberg
(1880–1915)

Philip
(1884–1957)
=
Eileen Rendall
(1893–1979)

Lancelot (Bunny)
(1886–1937)

Eileen (Kiddy)
(1888–1937)
=
Robert Macfarlane
(1868–1907)

Lionel (Diamond)
(1890–91)

Diana
(1917–2007)
=
Alexander Hay
(1911–84)

Gwyn Macfarlane
(1907–87)

Ben Hay
(b 1941)

ELSTREE HILL HOUSE SCHOOL
1848–1939

I shall continue to tell parents that, upon the whole and as far as I can judge, the best preparatory school in England is Elstree.
Dr J.E.C. Welldon, headmaster of Harrow, 1888

PART ONE

INTRODUCTION

It is a privilege to write a history of Elstree School, particularly given that my two sons attended the school. It is a chance to understand it better, and to chart the changes from the olden-day prep school ethos to its present incarnation. There is an adage that if you want to find out about something, you write a book about it, and it is in that spirit that I approach this assignment. I am grateful to the governors of the school for entrusting this task to me.

In 1979, the longstanding headmaster I.C.M. Sanderson produced a small book about the school, outlining its history from its origins until 12 August 1969, when he and his wife left Woolhampton for retirement in Lavenham, Suffolk. He was the third in a generation of Sandersons who had presided over the school, their tenure lasting for a century. His book was privately printed and called *A History of Elstree School and Three Generations of the Sanderson Family*. I have used his book as a bible. However, it would not be entirely unfair to suggest that the author was ailing as he finished his work, and that the story, told with such verve in the early pages, loses energy after 1945.

Richard Russell's *Elstree School, Woolhampton 1939–1989* carried the story forward, creating a good framework for the later years. The next headmaster, Terrence McMullen, was going to tackle the years from 1969 to 1995, for which he gathered notes from some old boys and former members of staff. The fruits of these notes have not been published until now. Some old boys were helpful, but a mailing to 800 of them was not as productive as he had hoped. Following this, Mr McMullen's health failed and he surrendered the task.

This book takes the story further. It does not intend to replace or supersede Ian Sanderson's book. He was part of the school's family and he lived through the years he described. Nevertheless, this book takes a slightly different approach, and I hope it sits comfortably beside its predecessor.

I did not attend the school myself, and so I come to it afresh. I am interested in how prep schools have changed over the years since I attended one between 1960 and 1964. Fortunately, I discovered early on that I knew Anthony Thomas, who was my French master at Scaitcliffe in Surrey, where he taught between 1959 and 1969, and also the late Richard Russell, a former headmaster of St George's School, Windsor, with whom I served as a lay steward at Windsor for many years.

As every parent knows, choosing a school for your child is a serious business. We looked at several, all of which had merit. One obvious reason for us choosing Elstree was that we lived nearby. However, the overriding reason was the way we were treated by the then headmaster, Syd Hill, on our first visit.

On a visit to another school (I exaggerate slightly to make my point), the headmaster greeted us in his study, almost with his feet on the desk, and told us: 'Sign up quickly, and now Jenkins will show you round.' Syd Hill, on the other hand, was waiting quietly in the hall. He showed us around the whole school personally, and we were thus able to see him interacting with the boys and staff, receiving an impression of the obvious respect they had for him. As the tour continued, he answered our questions and made the points he wished us to know about Elstree.

If ever I needed reassurance that we had chosen the right school, it came later when I witnessed the caring way the school coped with the tragedy of a young pupil dying of an inoperable brain tumour. To me, the sensitivity with which that was approached seemed unsurpassable.

Another thing that impressed me particularly was when Syd Hill told us that new boys were assigned a 'companion' to guide them into Elstree life, a concept introduced by Terrence McMullen. This new spirit of friendliness was markedly different to my day. I liked my school, but I was always a little wary and afraid, and I doubt I was alone in having this feeling. This change from fear to friendliness was more than welcome. Indeed, there have been times when school fathers have joked that they would not mind checking in to a school like Elstree themselves, brushing up their French, playing some music, having a run around the running track in the afternoon, a warm shower, building a fantastic model and then heading home. There are aspects of the modern prep school which compare well with a smart country club.

As we shall see, it was not ever thus. Commander Sanderson was a stern authoritarian who ran the school as he had previously commanded a ship in the Royal Navy. There were eccentric masters like Mr Hewitt, and a memorable team of school servants with their idiosyncratic expressions, leaving behind them a host of memories for the youngsters to take into adult life.

Evelyn Waugh said much for the schoolmasters of his day in *Decline and Fall* (1928). There is a scene early on when young Paul Pennyfeather is unfairly sent down for indecent behaviour. He goes to see the porter and tells him they are unlikely to see each other again for a long time. The porter comments: 'No, sir, and very sorry I am to hear about it. I expect you'll be becoming a schoolmaster, sir. That's what most of the gentlemen does, sir, that gets sent down for indecent behaviour.'[1]

As with so many schools where there is a headmaster, his/her family, a number of assistant masters, a matron and staff, not to mention a regular influx of boys/girls, the story inevitably produces a mixture of sterling characters who dedicate their lives to education, some less popular ones, and boys/girls whose lives veer from national, even international achievement, to mediocrity, and in some cases tragedy.

This book tells the story of Elstree from its early days through a variety of headmasters in holy orders, the Sanderson family who ran it for three generations, and its subsequent incarnation as a charitable trust. Some remarkable figures have passed through the doors at Elstree Hill and Woolhampton, and this book celebrates them too.

Fortunately, the days of loos with no doors, and one downstairs room for bathing are long past.

CHAPTER ONE

THE ENGLISH PREP SCHOOL

Preparatory schools have come to act as 'feeders' to public schools, but it was not always thus. Some of them were private classical schools and rivals to nineteenth-century public schools. They came in two types – either based on private enterprise or on philanthropy. Their origins can be traced back to the eighteenth century, and by the end of the nineteenth century, their role as a natural complement to the prosperous public school system was well established. Many were run by generations of the same family, and later developed as institutions run by charitable trusts. (This was the case with Elstree.)

Some prep schools prepared boys for public schools, others for the Royal Navy. A variety of such schools abounded and were to become known as 'preparatory' or 'private' schools, although some are referred to as 'quasi-preparatory'. Only in 1892 was the Association of Headmasters of Preparatory Schools established, at which time it was estimated that 400 or so could reliably be described as prep schools.

Many were run by indigent or scholastically minded clergymen, or by women (otherwise known as dames) who were forced to earn their own living. Donald Leinster-Mackay, who wrote the first proper history of prep schools, entitled *The Rise of the English Prep School* (1984), placed the great Dr Thomas Arnold (1795–1842) in the former category:

> The second propellant of the preparatory school was the indigent clergyman.
> As early as the eighteenth century they began to absent themselves from their
> parishes to become full-time private classical schoolmasters, preparing boys
> for entry to the universities.[2]

Some schools grew up around a rectory. Cheam, for example, developed as the brainchild of Revd William Gilpin, Vicar of Boldre in the New Forest, who became its headmaster in 1755 (though it did not become a full preparatory school until 1855). Then there were those assistant masters at public schools who were tempted to set up their own schools, maintaining good links with the public schools where they had taught previously. Revd Lancelot Sanderson fell into this category, having been an assistant master at Harrow, before becoming headmaster of Elstree in 1869. The need for prep schools gained strength when the public schools introduced entrance examinations. The great public schools, of which at one time there were considered to be nine (Eton, Winchester, Westminster, Charterhouse, St Paul's, Merchant Taylors', Harrow, Rugby, and Christ's Hospital), were followed by a great number of others in the late nineteenth century, including Cheltenham, Marlborough, Rossall, Wellington and Malvern.

Another factor in the creation of preparatory schools was the attitude of Dr Arnold, who was against the presence of younger boys in his school. He segregated the boys of eight and nine from the older boys, and when he abolished his Form 1 in 1837, the first purpose-designed prep school was born, Windlesham House, on the Isle of Wight, which later moved to Brighton.*

There is no doubt that the earliest prep schools were noted for harsh discipline and spartan conditions, something which is mercifully no longer the case. Many pupils left savage accounts in their memoirs. Lord Lawrence (1811–1879), later Viceroy of India, was apparently flogged every day of his school life at a school run by a certain Mr Gough (except one particular day when he was flogged twice). Charles Dickens was not exaggerating when he described the conditions of Dotheboys Hall in *Nicholas Nickleby* (1838), while *Tom Brown's Schooldays*, the 1857 novel

George du Maurier's sketch of school discipline

* There were, of course, many other schools that could claim to have existed before 1837.

7

by Thomas Hughes, painted a grim account of life at Dr Arnold's Rugby, which the author had attended between 1834 and 1842.

Whenever these schools are discussed, it is not long until the subject of corporal punishment arises. Books on Eton by Tim Card, and in particular a biography of the controversial Eton headmaster Anthony Chenevix-Trench by Mark Peel, inspired a barrage of letters to newspapers relating experiences with the cane and the birch from fascinated old boys.

Anthony Glyn, grandson of the famous Elinor Glyn (of tiger skin fame), left a memorable account of a sadistic headmaster in his novel *Kick Turn* (1963). The narrator's godfather, Revd Duncan Gregg, is headmaster of a prep school in Hampshire, and has a notice board headed '*Quicunque Flet*' ('Whoever weeps') with a baby's dummy pinned to it. Any boy caught crying had his name written on the board. Two grim vignettes from the book are worth repeating. The first was Glyn's description of the school miscreants:

> My godfather's study door was on the right, just before the green baize door, and outside it were five boys waiting. They always looked the same on these occasions; rather tense, yet casual, as if they had no special reason for being there, but merely paused to admire the wallpaper. They never met your eyes, and you never spoke to them. They were waiting to be beaten by my godfather.[3]

At that point, the narrator took a walk:

> I didn't want to be within earshot of my godfather's study, though probably there wouldn't be anything to hear; even more, I didn't want to be in the drawing-room when he came in afterwards, his soft blue eyes for once hard and bright, his voice a little louder than usual, fast and excited.[4]

Possibly even grimmer was the headmaster's response to the death of Ormisher, a boy with an aptitude for mathematics but wholly unsuited to climbing, who was forced to join the Easter climbing party to Pen-y-Pass. Ormisher proved unequal to the task and fell sixty feet, landed on his head, and died of a fractured skull. On the first Sunday of the summer term, the headmaster preached a sermon about Ormisher:

'I know we are all thinking this morning of someone who was with us last term and will not be with us again. But we must all realise, if we don't realise already, that these things just have to be. In our continual struggle to bring out true leaders everywhere, our struggle against cowardice and laziness, against a type of person who will always choose the easy way, against the treacherous idea of safety first, we must realise that there must always be some who fall' – he paused dramatically – 'by the wayside …'

'We must never regard human life as anything else but expendable. It exists to be spent, so that others may buy with it something valuable and important. When a Commander-in-Chief makes his plan of battle, he always writes down in his plan that he is prepared to accept a certain proportion of casualties, perhaps twenty-five per cent, thirty-three-and-a-third per cent, forty per cent, fifty per cent, whatever it may be. He never writes down nought per cent, because he knows quite well that if that was part of his plan he would never win his battle. So we must all be prepared to accept casualties. I must be prepared to accept them, and so must you. So that we can win our battle, win something great and valuable, without which our lives on this earth would have no importance or meaning at all.'[5]

The above may be fiction, but it sums up much of what was disagreeable about prep schools in those days.

In the first volume of his official life of Winston Churchill, his son Randolph quotes Roger Fry on corporal punishment at St George's School, Ascot, in the 1880s. It was Fry's unfortunate duty to hold boys down while they were birched by Mr Sneyd-Kynnersley:

In the middle of the room was a large box draped in black cloth and in austere tones the culprit was told to take down his trousers and kneel before the block, over which I and the other head boy held him down. The swishing was given with the master's full strength and it took only two or three strokes for drops of blood to form everywhere, and it continued for 15 or 20 strokes when the wretched boy's bottom was a mass of blood. Generally of course the boys endured it with fortitude but sometimes there were scenes of screaming, howling and struggling which made me sick with disgust …[6]

9

At my own prep school, Scaitcliffe, beatings were still carried out, and only ceased when the headmaster put his own son into the school and realised that he would not have the heart to beat him. My father recalled that on the first night of his first term there in 1921, his headmaster summoned several boys to his study and beat them because, on the last night of the summer term, the matron had discovered that they had plaited the tassels on their school blankets. My father also remembered the headmaster of Heatherdown standing on the side of the pitch, shouting at one of his boys who was not playing to standard: 'Jenkins! Swish!' And he gestured the swinging of a cane which would be his lot if he did not pull his act together. At Falconbury School in Surrey, one old boy recalled: 'Beatings would cease two weeks before the end of term, because the headmaster did not want to send boys home with bruising that would be evident to parents.'[7]

Bullying was another aspect of school life in the early days of prep and public schools, the masters actively encouraging it as a way of maintaining discipline. To 'sneak' (that is, to tell) on a bully even when I was at school in the 1960s would be to risk social ostracism that could follow you throughout life.

In 1905, the Hon. Henry Coke considered the changes in school life since he had attended Temple Grove School, a feeder for Eton:

> The luxury enjoyed by the present boy is a constant source of astonishment to us grandfathers. We were half starved, we were exceedingly dirty, we were systematically bullied, and we were flogged and caned as though the master's pleasure was in inverse ratio to ours.[8]

There is no doubt that prep schools have evolved and improved considerably in the last 100 years. It is impossible to alter human nature, but luckily it is possible to change what is acceptable or unacceptable in human behaviour. And that is the difference.

CHAPTER TWO

EARLY DAYS

Elstree School is currently located at the former Woolhampton House, not far from Reading. It has been there since 1939, and has thrived and developed beyond recognition in the last eighty-four years.

The original Elstree School dates from 1848, when it was situated at Hill House, a mansion in Elstree, Hertfordshire. Built in 1779, it had a huge chestnut tree (said to be 1,000 years old) outside the front door. Years later, it became a rehabilitation centre for men suffering from emotional and nervous disorders (being visited by Princess Marina, as Patron of the S.O.S. Society, in July 1963). Today, the building is a residential care home.

In those days, the school was set in an entirely rural landscape and remained so until the 1930s, when the Northern line on the London Underground was extended to Bushey Heath. Hill House stood at the top of a

The gardens at Elstree Hill House

The original Elstree School

steep hill just before the village of Elstree, long before it became famous for its film studio. It commanded a fine view across the Roman Watling Street to its playing fields, beyond which was a lake-like reservoir. There also stood a neglected monument commemorating the site of the Battle of Potter's Bar, where Queen Boadicea was killed by Roman invaders (now the A5 from London to Holyhead), and on fine days there is also a distant view of St Albans Abbey.

To the right of Watling Street stood a cluster of school buildings, which were added on in a miscellaneous way to the original manor house. The headmaster, meanwhile, had his own large house set in an equally large garden. To the north was the school yard. Former pupil Édouard Roditi described it as an 'arid expanse, flanked on the far side by a gymnasium that looked more like a kind of barn, and by an outdoor shed that housed two rows of sand-toilets. In winter these seemed to me, who had never yet seen anything but water-closets supplied with central heating, to be the world's coldest and draftiest privies, and in summer its most distressingly odoriferous.'[9]

12

The squash courts
at the old school

At the back of the yard were six open squash courts (with no back wall), and in later years there was a swimming pool and two grass tennis courts. During free time, balls were kicked up and down in a game called 'yard footer'.* On the other side of the road were the playing fields and later the Victorian Gothic red-brick school chapel. These were accessed by what Roditi called 'a narrow and damp underground tunnel that plunged beneath the Roman road, and thus avoided the dangers of its traffic',[10] which was constructed in 1907. To the north and west lay the open landscape of Hertfordshire, with the old de Havilland works in the distance.

In the early days of motor cars, a local farmer used to keep horses to pull them up the hill when their engines proved inadequate. Later, the boys would enjoy spotting a beautiful old steam truck that delivered beer to neighbouring public houses.

There had been some kind of educational establishment at Elstree Hill in the late 1700s, but only in 1842 can evidence be found that the Rudge family, who owned Hill House, leased it to Revd Evan Edgar Rowsell, 'who had a few pupils'. It would seem that one of these was the cartoonist and

---

* In the 1920s, balls that bounced over the wattle fencing into the road were recovered by Sam Rose, the bootman, who called the boys by their school numbers rather than their names: 'That there number 17 has lost his gym shoes.' Sam had a small hut at the lower end of the yard.

novelist George du Maurier (1834–1896), author of *Trilby*, whose family lived partly in Paris and partly in London. Elstree School thus existed before Charles Dickens wrote *Nicholas Nickleby*.

A Dickensian scene from *Nicholas Nickleby*

CHAPTER THREE

REVD LEOPOLD JOHN BERNAYS
(1820–1882)

HEADMASTER 1847–60

In 1847, the lease was taken over by Revd Leopold John Bernays (1820–1882), who settled there and became the first headmaster about whom anything is known. Born in 1820, he was the son of a German languages professor at King's College, London. He became a Fellow of St John's College, Oxford, and was recommended to take Elstree on by Dr Charles Vaughan, the headmaster of Harrow, in 1847. Bernays arrived at Elstree with a few pupils of his own and ran the school until 1860. Evidently popular as a clergyman, he was consid-

Revd Leopold John Bernays

ered a stern headmaster. Mary E. Richardson, writing about her brother, John Maunsell Richardson (1846–1912), recalled that he was 'not only renowned as a first-rate schoolmaster, but for his terrible temper – even foaming at the mouth at times, so it was said – and that he thrashed any offender with extraordinary mercilessness at the slightest provocation.'[11] Bernays had the habit of delivering himself of thundering sermons: 'Nothing can make life sweet and happy but a constant preparation for death' was an oft-repeated line.[12]

In one of his sermons, he blasted the small boys: 'If we could see the very jaws of hell open to receive us, and ourselves hastening madly down the road with nothing to arrest our career – how we should pray!' At times, he was evidently exasperated by his youthful flock, pondering on how 'one week passed amongst you pains me, with its long catalogue of idleness and carelessness, of disobedience and wilfulness, of harsh and profligate words.'[13]

Nevertheless, one old boy wrote of him: 'I maintain that with all the hard and severe discipline (and severe it was) still we ought to be grateful to those who turned out courteous, brave, high-minded English gentlemen from the school at Elstree Hill.'[14] A tragedy the headmaster had to suffer, albeit after he retired, was the loss of his eldest son, Ernest, who was drowned off the coast of Glengariff, Ireland on 31 August 1870.*

By the time Elstree became a school, it was housed in a large building behind a wall. The proximity of the road meant that there was always the noise of traffic, which kept some boys awake on summer evenings when windows were open. Before the road was tarred in 1909, the front of the house was regularly covered in dust. But there were occasional distractions – elephants passing by on their way to Whipsnade Zoo, the playing of barrel organs interrupting classroom studies and, in November 1852, the Scots Greys riding past to take part in the Duke of Wellington's state funeral.

In those days, the curriculum consisted mainly of classics, with a few lessons of mathematics each week and the occasional French lesson from a visiting French teacher. The school day began with prayers in the Big Schoolroom. Punishment involved the use of the 'Drill Book': for minor offences, a half-drill was ordered; for more serious offences, a whole drill. The administering of these punishments was supervised by either Sergeant Stubbs or Instructor Banks. On Sundays, everyone went under the subway to the chapel for two school services.

School colours were pink with white quarterings. Normal school dress was grey flannel trousers with grey sweaters. On Sundays, the boys wore suits with stiff Eton collars and in summer they wore grey 'floppers' (a kind of sun hat).

In the neighbourhood were rival schools – Lockers Park, Orley Farm, Evelyns and the Golden Parsonage. For cricket matches, the boys wore long

---

* Bernays Hall at Stanmore was built in Ernest's memory.

white trousers, with white shorts for soccer. (Eventually, the laundering of these became prohibitively expensive.)

In one cricket match, one of Revd Bernays's more famous pupils, Charles Montagu Doughty (1843–1926), who came to the school from Theberton Hall, Saxmundham, Suffolk, was hit in the face by a cricket ball. He made no mention of it, but his cheekbone was smashed and the scar showed for the remainder of his life. On another occasion, there was a competition to see who could stand on one leg the longest. Doughty started standing on one leg when his friends went to church; he was still there, and still on one leg, when they returned.

Doughty went on to be educated at a school for the navy in Portsmouth, followed by King's College, London, and Caius College, Cambridge. He was a reserved and serious figure, who sported a thick beard. He relished sixteenth-century literature and Teutonic languages, becoming well-known as a poet and traveller and authoring *Travels in Arabia Deserta* (1884). When he travelled in Arabia, he remained resolutely an Englishman and a Christian.

The school produced a number of celebrated old boys from the Bernays stable. One was Alexander Badcock (1844–1907), later General Sir Alexander Badcock, KCB, CSI, who came from a Taunton banking family. He went on to Harrow and served in various campaigns in India, including under Field Marshal Earl Roberts, and as Quartermaster General in India from 1895 to 1900.

Another was R.E.B. Crompton (1845–1940), who attended Elstree in 1856 and later attended Harrow. He became famous as an electrical engineer, pioneering electric lighting and public electricity supply systems. He was twice president of the Institution of Electrical Engineers, a Fellow of the Royal Society, and a founder member of the RAC.

George Ratcliffe Woodward (1848–1934) also went on to Harrow and then Gonville and Caius College, Cambridge (graduating third-class in the Classics Tripos), before becoming an Anglican priest. He is particularly remembered for writing religious verse, some of which he translated from Renaissance melodies.

In the next generation of old boys was John Whitehead (1860–1899), whose family lived in Wimbledon. Whilst attending the Edinburgh

Institution, the headmaster, Dr Ferguson, greatly encouraged his interest in natural history. Whitehead subsequently became an ornithologist and explorer, but developed a weakness of the lungs during one of his travels and spent the winter of 1881/82 in the Engadin, Switzerland. The following winter he travelled to Corsica to search for different birds, discovering an unknown breed, the Corsican nuthatch. His later travels included a collecting trip to Mount Kinabalu, North Borneo, which lasted from October 1884 to August 1888. His discoveries of animals and birds were recorded in his book, *Exploration of Mount Kina Balu* (1893).

In January 1899, Whitehead set off once more in the direction of the Philippines, but was frustrated by the war between the USA and Spain. Presently, he sailed for Hong Kong in a bid to explore the island of Hainan, but fever set in. With some difficulty he made his way back to the coast, dying at the port of Hoi-hou on 2 June.

A couple of years younger was J. Bruce Ismay (1862–1937). Ismay was chairman of the White Star Line, which owned the ill-fated *Titanic*. At school, he was particularly fond of football and lawn tennis. He was aboard the maiden voyage of the *Titanic* to New York in April 1912 when it hit an iceberg. After the collision, Ismay helped women and children into lifeboats for two hours, and when at last he got into a collapsible boat, there were no passengers in sight. Because some 1,500 passengers drowned (including the captain, Edward Smith) while he

J. Bruce Ismay

survived, his reputation was greatly damaged, though he was cleared in Lord Mersey's report on the disaster. He made amends by establishing the Mercantile Marine Fund, providing £19,000 (including £1,000 of his own money) for the benefit of seamen's widows.[15] When he died in 1937, every flag in Liverpool flew at half-mast.

Sir Felix Cassel (1869–1953), nephew of Sir Ernest Cassel, was a top lawyer who became Judge Advocate-General and was created a baronet. Like so many others, he went on to Harrow, and later to Corpus Christi

College, Oxford with a scholarship. His father lived in Orme Square, just off the Bayswater Road.

The Influence of Harrow

Harrow was only a few miles from Elstree, situated on the same hill. Due to the proximity, a strong link was forged between these two educational establishments. Revd Bernays was a friend of the poet Matthew Arnold, son of Dr Thomas Arnold, the legendary headmaster of Rugby. Indeed, there is a strong educational tradition at Elstree that extends directly from Dr Arnold through several generations of headmasters. Arnold was the man who revolutionised the public school system, introducing boarding houses, prefects (with the right to cane younger boys), organised games, and stressing the importance of the development of a boy's character. These schools remained stern establishments for many generations to come, but it is fair to say that he introduced a strong Christian ethic into the school system. Lytton Strachey wrote of him: 'By introducing morals and religion into his scheme of education, he altered the whole atmosphere of Public School life.'[16] This ethic was followed to the letter by three subsequent headmasters of Harrow, namely Dr Charles Vaughan, Dr H. Montagu Butler and Dr J.E.C. Welldon, all of whom were closely involved with Elstree.

The Bernays' time at Elstree more or less coincided with the period during which the celebrated Revd Dr Charles Vaughan was headmaster of Harrow. Vaughan and Bernays got on well, and between them they established Elstree as a feeder for Harrow, a link that was maintained well into the 1950s. Vaughan often visited the school and examined the boys for entry to Harrow. Indeed, in 1858 the school was even being advertised as 'the Harrow Preparatory School at Elstree'.

Dr Vaughan (1816–1897) had been taught by Arnold at Rugby. He took on the headmastership of Harrow in 1844 when he was twenty-eight years old. At the time, it was at a low ebb, with only sixty boys attending. By the time he left, however, there were 469 students. His mission was to revivify studies and discipline. He chose good teachers, including his successor, Dr Montagu Butler, and Sir George Trevelyan, and is remembered for concentrating more on the importance of teaching than school administration. It was written of him: 'As teacher, his main object was to impart to his pupils that strict accuracy of thought and expression, and to the more capable of them that keen sense of style and the subtle delicacies of language, in which his own delight particularly lay.'[17] He remained headmaster until 1859, when he resigned amidst laudatory speeches, farewell dinners and so forth. Four years later, he was offered the Bishopric of Rochester, but declined it.

Vaughan's reluctance to take a new post was unexplained for many years. As recently as 1964, however, the truth emerged. Pressure had been put on him by Dr J.A. Symonds, father of the poet and writer John Addington Symonds, on account of Vaughan's affair with a boy at the school called Alfred Pretor, as well as other unsavoury activities. As Jonathan Gathorne-Hardy wrote: 'Few falls have been as swift, as catastrophic and as complete.'[18]

Dr H. Montagu Butler (1833–1918) took over at Harrow at the age of twenty-six. His father had been head-master before him, and he had been a pupil at Harrow under Vaughan. He was a traditionalist who nevertheless made reforms in science and music, and got along well with both boys and masters. The biographer Walter Sichel wrote lines about him which say much for the mindset of schoolmasters at that time: 'Butler was anything but a pedagogue, yet neither was he the cruel humanitarian who spares the rod.'[19] He was a bearded figure, and

Dr H. Montagu Butler

in later life, as Master of Trinity College, Cambridge, he not only sported a thick white beard but also wore a skullcap.

Butler was followed by Dr J.E.C. Welldon (1854–1937), a Fellow of King's College, Cambridge, who predicted enigmatically that he was most likely to be remembered in history as Winston Churchill's headmaster.[20] A friend of George Curzon and Edward Lyttelton, he was headmaster of

Harrow between 1885 and 1898. An auto-cratic administrator and imposingly tall at 6 feet 5 inches, he was known as 'The Porker' by the boys. He was a lifelong bachelor who enjoyed the 'close companionship of a manservant, Edward Hudson Perkins from whose death in 1932 he never recovered.' While at Harrow, he was commended for having ruled the school 'with the masterly force of an infectious personality'.[21] He was appointed Bishop of Calcutta in 1898.

Dr J.E.C. Welldon

In due course, one of the highlights of the Elstree school year was the annual Eton versus Harrow match at Lord's. There were eighty boys at the school, and about half of them would be taken to the match, often by their parents in their cars. Years later, Ian Sanderson still took boys to the match.

CHAPTER FOUR

REVD THOMPSON PODMORE
(1823–1895)

HEADMASTER 1860–9

In 1860, Revd Thompson Podmore took over as headmaster of Elstree, having been Bernays' partner there for a decade. He only lasted nine years. He was the father of six children, including Frank Podmore (1856–1910), the spiritualist, writer on psychical research, and a founding member of the Fabian Society, who was born at the school and educated there (1863–8), before winning a scholarship to Haileybury College.*

Podmore worked closely with Harrow's headmaster, Dr Montagu Butler, though it would seem that Butler eventually lost confidence in him. Podmore presided over a phase during which the number of pupils declined. He purchased the freehold of the school in 1864, but by 1869 he was in financial difficulty. His wife was said to be particularly extravagant. Eventually, Dr Butler decided there should be a change, and Podmore went off to be headmaster of Eastbourne College, where things went better for

Revd Thompson Podmore

---

* Frank Podmore was 'found drowned' in the New Pool at Malvern. By a strange coincidence, another son, Austin Podmore, died on 17 October 1937, the same day as Bruce Ismay.

him. He grew sandy whiskers, became very thin, and walked with both of his hands resting on his hip bones.

In 1885, he retired to a rectory near Rugby. Walking to the station at Daventry, Northamptonshire to catch a train to London for the Old Eastbournian dinner on 9 January 1895, he collapsed and was found dead in the snow at the age of seventy-one.

CHAPTER FIVE

REVD LANCELOT SANDERSON
(1838–1904)

HEADMASTER 1869–1900

Revd Lancelot Sanderson was born in Lancaster on 24 March 1838, the second son of Lancelot Sanderson (1802–1871) and his wife, Agnes Winder. His father, a schoolmaster at the Royal Lancaster Grammar School came from Morland, Westmorland, and had known poverty when he was young. Revd Lancelot was the first of three generations of Sandersons who would take on the headmastership of Elstree School. The three men were all remarkably tall and handsome, all polished classical scholars with charming manners and elegant taste. Revd Lancelot had side whiskers. Édouard Roditi, at the school from 1919,

Revd Lancelot Sanderson

commended all the Sandersons for instilling into the pupils a love of Gibbon and Macaulay, the poetry of Byron and Tennyson, and the 'vigorous poems' of Charles Kingsley and Henry Newbolt.[22]

Lancelot Sanderson went up to Clare College, Cambridge with a scholarship in classics, and in 1862 took holy orders, serving as curate and senior tutor in Upton, Torquay, under Revd George Townsend Warner (1815–1869), whose daughter, Katherine Susan Oldfield Warner (1843–1921), he

24

married in the autumn of 1864. She was always known at the school as 'Mrs Kitty'. It is said she took one look at him and declared that he was the man for her. They were different in temperament – she full of enthusiasm and merriment, he reserved, controlled, dignified and with a ponderous manner. One of his expressions was 'a little truth can often be the biggest lie'. He believed strongly in truth and honesty, compelled his family and schoolboys to think before they spoke, and thus did not create an easy atmosphere around him. He took life seriously and he seldom relaxed.

Sanderson taught at Harrow for a time before taking Elstree on in 1869 and running it with supreme efficiency thereafter. In taking the school over from Podmore, he needed £2,000, but was £500 short. Greatly impressed by Revd Lancelot, Dr Butler made up the shortfall, thus establishing the Sandersons at Elstree for the next 100 years. Revd Lancelot took fifty boys who were too young for Harrow with him to the new school.

School group, 1870

The new headmaster, known affectionately as 'the Guv', was clean-shaven in a generation of beards. He was a keen sportsman. During his headmastership, the school was run as a family show, with three of his brothers – Tylecote, Charles and Henry – all resident teachers. Another brother, Edward, occasionally taught mathematics. Both Henry and Edward were first-class cricketers. Revd Sanderson's elder brother, John Sanderson, JP (1831–1908), became a banker and sent his son, another Lancelot, to the school.* Three of his sisters had taught in schools in Lancashire.

Staff, 1870

F.B. Wilson wrote of the headmaster: 'In the year 1890 there can have been no private school in the world that was quite on a par with Elstree, if only by reason of the wonderful selection of masters whom the Revd Lancelot Sanderson, MA, got together.' Wilson continued: 'He loved his school heart and soul, and nothing was quite good enough for him; as far as the school went he would have attempted to improve on perfection.'[23] Amongst other things, Sanderson agreed for six squash courts to be built. His wife's great-niece, the novelist Sylvia Townsend Warner, left a fictional description of him:

> His attitude, as he leans, in his long sleek clerical coat and well-cut clerical
> waistcoat, on the back of a chair looking down on the open book in his hand,

---

* John's son, Rt Hon. Sir Lancelot Sanderson (1863–1944), was educated at Elstree, later becoming a barrister, Conservative MP for Appleby, Chief Justice of the High Court of Judicature in Calcutta, a member of the Judicial Council of the Privy Council, and an occasional county cricketer, who played two first-class matches – once for Lancashire (1884) and once for the Marylebone Cricket Club (MCC) (1888).

26

emphasises his graceful build and port. Pensive, elegant, high-minded, he looks like a stanza in 'In Memoriam'; and it would seem well-nigh inevitable (though in fact nothing of the kind occurred) that the Church of England would lead onwards into becoming a bishop …[24]

He rented a lodge at Inverpolly in Sutherland for a family holiday with the older children each summer, and loved to shoot and fish there. Back at Elstree, he took care of the scholastic side of the school, while Mrs Kitty was a considerable asset in her own right. She had a natural ease with boys and young masters; with her high spirits, charm and informality, she became the confidante and source of encouragement to many. As one of her grandsons, Tim Brierly, recalled:

At Elstree the boys called her 'Mrs Kitty'. She used to go round the dormitories and kiss each boy goodnight. She was never happier than in a crowded room. She loved entertaining at School functions at which everyone was charmed by her gaiety and the genuine warmth of her greeting. Servants adored her. Her correspond-

ence was immense. She would exert herself without stint on behalf of anyone in trouble. I remember her when she was old and a widow, arthritic, nearly blind and in very reduced circumstances, worrying about the welfare of the Klondike miners as if she had no worries of her own.

She knew sorrow and defeat as well as success but her courage never failed. Not only had she the school to look after and thirteen of her own extremely lively children to bring up, but she found room in her affections for her children's friends as they grew up.[25]

Mrs Kitty was elegant. Her daughter Agnes used to wait for her to come and say good night before she went down to dinner:

> She was like the Princess of Wales in her black dress by Debenham, with its long train. Bracelets on slender wrists, and a diamond bee which she wore on a black velvet ribbon round her throat. She carried herself so beautifully and always smelt of fresh violets. Even if she had none to wear she used a little whiff of true violet scent.[26]

Mrs Kitty was also semi-invalid; she felt the cold badly and frequently lay on the sofa near a roaring fire. She drew people to her like a magnet, and they poured out their hearts to her. One day, the bald clergyman, Mr Fincher, prostrated himself at her feet, talking gibberish until he suddenly pulled himself together. Mrs Kitty had a brother known to the family as 'Uncle Townsend'. He played great games with the children, and his vigilant wife kept an eye on him to make sure he only had one glass of port after dinner.

Mrs Kitty kept an eye on the young masters, serving them port or tea if they had colds. One master, C.P. Wilson, known in the family as 'St Christopher', sometimes carried Mrs Kitty upstairs when she was not allowed to walk. He had a cricket blue from Cambridge, a soccer blue, and the distinction of captaining the rugby side, playing centre half for England. The boys loved to be coached in football by him. He was also a fine classical scholar, a strong swimmer, a fine skater, a good tennis player and he sang well.

The wives of Harrow masters were inevitably regular visitors, one of them, Mrs Stogdon, stomping in with a wooden leg. Many Harrow masters sent their sons to Elstree on favourable financial terms.

The Sanderson family lived formally, guests processing into special dinners arm in arm. Every summer they gave a big party with a concert, performed by the school choir and the orchestra under the guidance of the music master, David Beardwell, a round, red-faced man who taught the boys well. Near to the school was the Elms, once the home of the actor William Macready (1793–1873), and then occupied by Revd Lancelot's sister, Sarah Watson.

The nursery was opposite Mrs Kitty's room and had a beautiful Queen Anne window overlooking the cricket field, some tall elms and the distant reservoir. From this room, many newly born Sandersons were brought out, the latest of the sixteen children born to Lancelot and Kitty, carried in the arms of the plump nurse, Mrs Bindon. Mrs Kitty's philosophy was that there was a loving, shining heaven full of angels with fluffy wings taking care of her ever-increasing flock, but this was balanced by a fierce nanny who believed in fear as her governing force.

Good observers of the family were John Galsworthy (1867–1933), later famous as the author of *The Forsyte Saga*, and his sister, Mabel. The Galsworthy family lived not far from Elstree. Lancelot Sanderson's young son Ted, who took over as headmaster some years later, had been at Harrow with Galsworthy, but Galsworthy had gone on to Oxford while Ted went to Cambridge. It was at that point, despite the different universities, that they became considerable friends.

John Galsworthy

Soon after coming down from Oxford, he became a regular at Elstree. He wrote a play for them called *Gipsy John*, which the younger Sandersons performed on the school stage. Galsworthy found the Sanderson family living in a rambling old house, where friends constantly dropped in for a meal or stayed the night. Mabel Sanderson, one of Ted's sisters, said 'they all loved Jack', but Agnes was not immediately impressed:

> He arrived, immaculately dressed complete with monocle. Without his monocle he was practically blind and it was a real necessity, and not merely worn for swank as we thought. His manner so gentle and refined, and his voice soft and weak, we mistook for feebleness. We summed him up as 'impossible.'[27]

Ted wrote that his siblings teased and ragged Galsworthy mercilessly as 'no good'. They once pushed him fully clothed into the swimming pool, an adventure he accepted without loss of temper. They introduced him to a game of hockey in the dining hall, 'a very strenuous game with canes and a tennis ball. It was no joke to be whacked on the legs with a biting cane or across the toes if you had slippers on'. They dropped his monocle into the tadpole bowl and sought to get him at their mercy. But Galsworthy passed these tests. He was fine when his horse stumbled in the field and he lost all his gold sovereigns in the hay; he acted in the Christmas plays and came to enjoy the intellectual atmosphere also provided by the Sanderson household.

Galsworthy took to corresponding with Monica, the eldest Sanderson daughter, remembered for her 'vivid loveliness' and 'intellectual vigour', and of whom it was said: 'She used to sing in her cold bath.' Monica was thus an early inspiration in Galsworthy's literary career, as he explored his writing skills in letters to her, some surviving from the south of France, Scotland and Westmorland in 1894.[28] At that time, no one thought he would be a writer.

Mabel Galsworthy left a good account of life at the school. She found the headmaster dedicated to his work and delicate in health, so not often seen by visitors. Mrs Kitty, on the other hand, was 'as young as any of her daughters in their teens and a truly amazing woman'.[29] Mabel loved her bird-like chatting. The family invariably sat down in their private dining room with twelve or fifteen at the table, and a further host of young Sandersons in the nursery upstairs. The family never failed to offer a visitor a bed for the night, 'though the bed might be a hard one, creaky and lumpy, in some little bare room with a queer name in any god-forsaken part of that capacious, rambling old house.'[30]

Lily Galsworthy, another sister, introduced George Sauter (1866–1937), a German artist, to the family. He was evidently a rather fierce-looking man with a huge nose and chin and penetrating blue eyes. He painted a portrait of Agnes and later married Lily, somewhat to the shock of the Galsworthy family.

When Ted went off to the South African War in 1900, there was a cooling between him and Galsworthy, since both Galsworthy and Joseph Conrad (of whom more later) were decidedly against this endeavour.

The Sixteen Sandersons

Mabel Galsworthy recalled that the thirteen Sandersons that survived were a picturesque crowd: 'half of them fair, with very light hair; most of the rest with hair that was nearly black; some of them strikingly handsome, and not one really plain one amongst the lot!'[31] The school echoed with boisterous laughter and games intermingled with intellectual conversation. Sylvia Townsend Warner described her cousins in fiction:

> Though the dear girls were beautiful, graceful, talented, warm-hearted, dressed in the height of fashion, and fervently religious, they were none of them gentle. A friend of the family said that when they came into the room, all lovely and all talking at once, it was like being descended on by a flight of angels. Angels in flight are not gentle. They sweep on their way, each angel single-mindedly bent on what it means to do next.[32]

The Sanderson children were raised in and around the school, and were a strong feature in school life. The third sister, Agnes Ridgeway (1874–1943), wrote a delightful and unpublished memoir of their family life from which it is possible to get a full, considered and sympathetic picture of the characters of the different siblings. Known as Totty or Totte, in 1908 she married a man eight years her junior, Revd Neville Ridgeway (1883–1973), who was teaching for a while at Elstree. He went on to be a schoolmaster at Tonbridge, running Ferox Hall, to which Joseph Conrad sent his son, John.

Of these children, the first one, Wyndham Lancelot Sanderson, was born at Harrow and died on the same day in 1865. Edward Lancelot (Ted) (1867–1939) would go on to become headmaster. (Of him, more will be discussed in Chapter Nine.)

Taking the other thirteen in order, there was Katherine Elizabeth Sanderson (another Kitty – or Kit) (1868–1887), who was virtually engaged to Ted Butler (1866–1948), Dr Montagu Butler's son. The next was (John) Murray Sanderson (1871–1935), also known as J.M. He was autocratic as a youngster and liked to be the leader of the siblings. If he wanted to be free of them on their Scottish holiday, he would retreat to a secret place of his own on the side of a mountain. He died in New South Wales.

Then there was Monica Sydney Sanderson (Mon) (1872–1934), very much the belle of the ball, and oblivious to the admiration she inspired. Dudley Barker wrote of her in 1963: 'Even now there are elderly men in London who can remember the vivid loveliness and the intellectual vigour of Monica Sanderson.'[33] And even Montague Rhodes James,[*] something of a misogynist, was impressed by her physical beauty. She married one of the assistant masters, Revd F. de W. Lushington, a one-time headmaster of the school, in 1899.

Following Agnes, the other children were Henry George Hallam Sanderson (King, Kingie or Hal) (1875–1940), who suffered spasms and became highly strung after a bout of whooping cough. Once, they nearly lost him over a cliff in Scotland. Then there was a serious accident in the school gymnasium when he fell from a trapeze, hurting himself. This caused a further change in his character. Agnes wrote that he developed into 'a rare character of loving kindness and beauty'.[34] He became a gunner during the First World War and suffered a poisoned wound in the leg. He lived for music, became an organist (taught by Billy Beardwell), and died at Eton.

Geraldine Margaret Sanderson (Gerry) (1877–1951) was considered most original. An attractive brunette, she could have been a good musician, but she preferred horses and dogs and spent any free time she had riding the colts across the fields. She married Henry Leeds Harrison.

Violet Meredith Sanderson (Vie) (1878–1953) was the most intelligent of all the daughters. She had a superb memory and could quote Dickens extensively by the age of six. She was a good violinist, but realising that she would never be first-class, she gave it up and became a hospital nurse.

Francis Grey Oke Sanderson (Grey) (1879–1947) began life with rickety legs and had to wear irons. He suffered a bad stammer, but also had inexhaustible energy. A rebellious child, he enrolled as a pupil in the school despite being too young. Unfortunately, on his first day there, another boy served him some tinned salmon and he developed ptomaine poisoning, from which he nearly died. He would often miss sport whilst he was at Harrow, and on returning to the school, created a great fuss by shooting C.P. Wilson's beautiful Persian cat in his garden. Soon after the incident, Wilson moved on to Sandroyd School. Grey rose to become a Lieutenant Colonel in the Indian Army.

---

[*] Montague Rhodes James, OM (1862–1936), otherwise known as M.R. James, is best-remembered as a writer of excellent antiquarian ghost stories, many placed in a contemporary setting. He was also Provost of King's College, Cambridge, and famously of Eton.

And then there were the little ones in the family. Flora (1881–1952) and Angela (Angie) (1883–1959) both had golden hair, bright colouring and blue eyes. Flora was sensitive, whereas Angie was lively and full of cheek. Flora had piano lessons from Matilde Verne. She married John Douglas Hoare, and Angie married Howard Goldberg.

Next came two more boys. First was Philip (Phil or Brucie) (1884–1957), who was wounded in Mesopotamia. He went on to marry Eileen Rendall, niece of Montague Rendall (1862–1950), the famous headmaster of Winchester. Next came Lancelot (Bunny) (1886–1916), who died in Berbera, British Somaliland. Eileen (Kiddy) (1888–1937) came next, and was possibly the most interesting of the youngsters. A born actress, she fascinated Galsworthy. She married Robert Gray Macfarlane; their son, Gwyn Macfarlane, CBE, FRS (1907–1987) became a famous haematologist. With her brothers, Phil and Bunny, they formed a fascinating trio.

The youngest child was Lionel (1890–1891), known as 'Diamond'. A godson of Lionel Ford, his sister Agnes called him 'a darling little fellow'. But he was invariably in pain. He was treated by the same doctor who had looked after Kit, but he never improved. He died when he was only a few months old. Summing up the life of this family, Agnes concluded on an optimistic note:

My mother created that happiness for her children, as mothers can. The Real World of the future will be built upon the foundation of family love, so that happiness will once more be universal. If every family was happy, what a radiant world the world would be.[35]

* * * * *

The eldest boy, Ted, who would eventually take over as headmaster, went to Harrow, where he was popular and won many prizes. He won a scholarship and was head of his house. At one time, he had a breakdown from overwork. He then went up to King's College, Cambridge, where he was a member of the T.A.F. Club (a drinking club so named because they met twice a fortnight). There exists a photograph of him seated next to the novelists E.F. Benson and M.R. James, E.H. Douty (later a surgeon), Hon. Marcus Dimsdale (translator of Livy and a Fellow of King's) and R. Carr

The T.A.F. Group.
BACK ROW:
G. Duckworth,
M. Sanderson,
H. Benson,
J.K. Stephen,
W. Crum &
W. Headlam
FRONT ROW:
E.L. Sanderson,
E.F. Benson,
M.R. James,
E.H. Douty,
M. Dimsdale &
R.C. Bosanquet

Bosanquet (archaeologist), with Gerald Duckworth, the publisher and half-brother of Virginia Woolf, Murray Sanderson (Ted's brother), Hugh Benson (later a Catholic priest), J.K. Stephen,* Walter Crum (later known as Sir Erskine Crum, formerly an Oxford rowing blue) and Walter Headlam (the Greek scholar) standing behind them.

Many of these names are something to conjure with, even in 2023. Some went on to be important educationalists, and it is thus reassuring to learn that, in 1889, in a scene that could have come from *Brideshead Revisited*, Francis Ford,† brother of Lionel Ford, future headmaster of Harrow, and other highly respectable undergraduates, including Ted Sanderson, placed Robert Ross (literary executor to Oscar Wilde) in King's College fountain. As Monty James recalled: 'They had talked about it for some time before

---

* J.K. Stephen (1859–1892) was a poet, tutor to Prince Albert Victor, Duke of Clarence (who spent some time at Cambridge), and a cousin of Virginia Woolf. He died of 'mania' in St Andrew's Hospital, Northampton.

† Francis Ford (1866–1940) became a master at Elstree on account of his being a Cambridge cricket blue, a left-handed batsman, and for his charm. Monica and Agnes Sanderson both fell in love with him, but in 1906 he married an attractive rich widow, Ethel Marion Stephenson. He played first-class cricket for Middlesex, Cambridge and the Marylebone Cricket Club. He also played in five Test matches in England and toured Australia in 1894–95. He was nicknamed 'Stork' on account of his height.

and the idea pleased me a good deal, but I was rather afraid of the consequences, and hoped it had blown over.'[36]

Ted rode a penny-farthing at Cambridge, visiting the cathedrals of the Loire on it in the company of Monty James. He once hurt himself badly after falling from it, and Francis Ford had to look after him. There were the usual youthful ventures into love. In his early life, he fell in love with Mary Leaf, whose brothers were at the school. She had beautiful grey eyes, and was a fine painter in watercolours as well as a good pianist. The siblings hoped she would marry Ted, but she turned him down, leaving him sorrowful and remote for a long period of time. According to his sister Agnes:

> He hid his feelings from us, and would not talk about his sufferings. I suppose it was natural that he thought us too young to understand, but we saw in his face and manner what he was going through and it was pain for us not to be able to help him. I remember going for walks over the moor with him, me hanging on his arm as being the only way of getting near him, and not saying a word to one another.[*][37]

M.R. James alarmed himself by being attracted to Stella Duckworth, sister of his Cambridge friend Gerald, while on a visit to Cornwall. She had many suitors, including J.K. Stephen. Ted became 'inflamed' with her, and James had to comfort him when the romance floundered.[†] Monty James continued to be a frequent visitor to Elstree, enjoying the boisterous family life there.

Ted trained for the church, but his constitution was damaged by too much rowing and running at Cambridge. He suffered from weak lungs, so he never took holy orders. Instead, he

M.R. James

was ordered to take a long sea voyage to Australia and New Zealand.

---

* Mary Leaf received many proposals but never married. She devoted herself to social work in the slums.

† Stella Duckworth (1869–1897), half-sister of Virginia Woolf, married John Hills, a lawyer, in 1897, but died of peritonitis during pregnancy soon afterwards.

John Galsworthy, meanwhile, had developed and matured on account of spending time with the Sanderson family. He was studying at the Chancery Bar but his father wanted him to switch to the Admiralty division, as he thought a sea voyage would be a help.[38] So, in November 1892, he joined Ted and they set off to tour Australia, New Zealand and the South Seas, their mission being to meet Robert Louis Stevenson in Samoa, for whom they both had 'a profound admiration'.[39] They reached Albany in Australia but were unable to get a boat to Samoa, so dropped that idea, and went instead to New Caledonia and the Fiji Islands. Sanderson recalled: 'At night we sat under Flamboyant trees and listened to the Convict band; and most beautifully those convicts played. The day or two we spent there made a great impression on Jack, who afterwards made use of some of the stories we heard there.'[40]

Ted kept an account of this trip, which his son, Ian, later transcribed. In this, he recorded how mosquitos got into the screen: 'It was like sleeping in a bee hive … Sleeping head and tails, J. & I kicked each other in the face periodically from the chagrin of mosquito poison.'[41]

Galsworthy proved a curious travelling companion. If he decided to jump across a brook, he invariably fell in. He was forever afraid of being late, he was convinced that all natives encountered were infected by disease, and if confronted with a tin that needed to be opened at the side, he opened it at the top: 'If the tin contained jam, poor Jack was sure to put it in the packing case upside down: so that the contents flowed in a sticky stream into anything which could least stand contact with the sticky.'[42]

During an excursion into the bush, Ted came down with a high fever and a bad attack of dysentery. Despite his impracticality, Galsworthy saved Ted's life by feeding him on porridge and a chicken leg for broth (stuffing the entire leg into a large kettle until it dwindled to the sufficient liquid required). He got a runner to head to the coast for dysentery medicine, and eventually Ted was slung into a litter of wattle, supported on a long bamboo pole and carried by four men for many miles, once for twenty-eight miles in one day. Impressively, despite crossing numerous bodies of water, he was only dropped twice, and never in a river. As he wrote later: 'Thanks mainly to Jack's infinite care, I got down alive.'[43]

In March 1893, they boarded *Torrens*, a fast sailing ship, for the return voyage to Britain. They met the first mate whilst he was busy loading cargo, a thin, dark man with long arms, broad shoulders and a strong accent. The voyage took fifty-six days, during which time Ted and Galsworthy listened to the mate's twenty years of tales, as he talked of life rather than literature. By contrast, the first mate recalled how inept the two men were as travellers, leaving their porthole open, losing books and clothes when the weather became rough and the sea rushed into their cabin. The first mate was Joseph Conrad (1857–1954). He had a half-finished manuscript with him, which Ted encouraged him to finish. Galsworthy wrote to his family:

Joseph Conrad

> The first mate is a Pole called Conrad and is a capital chap, though queer to look at; he is a man of travel and experience in many parts of the world, and has a fund of yarns on which I draw freely. He has been right up the Congo and all around Malacca and Borneo and other out of the way parts, to say nothing of a little smuggling in the days of his youth.[44]

Ted invited Conrad to stay at Elstree, and there began an important new phase for the young writer.

During the 1890s, although Revd Sanderson's health began to fail, Elstree School was filled with exciting figures, many of them friends of Ted's down from university. The boys had the chance of observing men of talent such as M.R. James, John Galsworthy and Joseph Conrad enjoying friendship with a host of young Sandersons on the brink of distinguished careers. Of the young Conrad, Agnes observed:

> A striking personality, and very courtly. 'How do you do?' meant more than that. With feet clapped together he bowed from the waist raising our hands to his lips and kissing them. I received a shock when he did that to me for the first time! I had never experienced such a thing. I felt horribly gauche … We called him 'Mr Conrad' … He could not have been old when we met

him but his rugged face made him appear old. At times it was full of sadness. His great dark eyes filled with brooding misery, such misery that one felt nothing could alleviate a deep-seated pain. He had known the agony of his dearest relatives suffering and dying at the hands of the Russians. No one could mention Russia without his face becoming purple with anger, and we learnt to be careful about that. Until we got to know him better he was a rather terrifying person.[45]

Conrad was a frequent visitor, staying at the school for ten days in April 1894 and again in March 1895. Mrs Kitty took a strong motherly interest in him, becoming his confidante and finding his English prose already highly proficient. Jack and Mabel also advised on the manuscript of *Almayer's Folly*, his first published novel. Following its publication, Conrad's writing career took off. He dedicated *Outcast of the Islands* to Ted in 1896, and when he published *The Mirror of the Sea* in 1906, he dedicated it to Katherine Sanderson, 'whose warm welcome and gracious hospitality, extended to the friend of her son, cheered the first days of my parting with the sea.'[46] He inscribed her personal copy as from 'her affectionate friend'.

Ted Sanderson with Oboe, *c*.1896

Conrad also used to enjoy the friendship between Galsworthy and Ted's brother Philip (Brucie). He observed Philip 'dancing in into the dining room one evening and talking to Galsworthy about his work. Not play – work. And he struck me then as a charming creature having a bright light of his own.'[47]

Conrad was also closely involved in the process of Ted marrying Helen Watson, the eldest of five daughters of the Sheriff-Substitute of Dumfries and Galloway: 'The platform of Elstree station is becoming for me a sort of hallowed ground. There you talked to me of your engagement and showed me the ring. I felt what a great part you and yours have played in my life.'[48]

As demonstrated, Ted had been greatly in love with Stella Duckworth some years before. In October 1896, Ted was about to set off to propose to Helen. Conrad encouraged him and urged him to put any doubts aside. Later, he put the case to Helen, who was afraid that marriage would be too quiet a life for Ted. All went well, and Ted married Helen in 1898.

After their marriage, the couple settled down at St Mary's, Elstree. They were both deeply religious, with Helen considered a woman of moral and intellectual vigour. Conrad described her as 'the presiding genius of good fortune'.[49] In due course, they had a son, Ian, followed by two daughters. Conrad remained a faithful correspondent with Ted for many years afterwards, telling him of his progress and discussing his work with him. However, he did not send his son to the school.

The Garden

Elstree had a beautiful garden with a substantial old holm oak, standing on a high bank overlooking the lower lawn. The garden proved a good hiding place for the children. On Sunday afternoons, the Sanderson children lay there as their mother read to them from Walter Scott, Dickens or Thackeray. There was a pink may tree, a skinny fir tree and a long elm avenue, which ended up the hill with a series of twisted pines. The avenue was the scene of many family adventures. There was a kitchen garden and a much-loved corner of the garden with a wall covered in sweet jasmine and a Virginia creeper. The Sanderson children were horrified to return after one summer holiday to find this shaded area swept away and replaced by three new squash courts for the boys. Clearly good for the school, this meant that the garden was now somewhat exposed, open to the road and the schoolyard.

Sport

Elstree was renowned among prep schools for its standard of cricket, largely due to the influence of Revd Sanderson. One of the first things the then headmaster did when he took over in 1869 was to enlarge the school cricket pitch. Following this, he enlisted cricket blues on to his staff and employed two bowling professionals from Lord's to coach the boys. Between 1877 and 1900, Elstree boys took part in seventy-seven Eton versus Harrow

Cricket team,
*c.*1920

matches at Lord's. Amongst the masters he employed were some ace cricketers, notably Ernest Smith, described as 'about as unpleasant a bowler on
the Elstree ground as any batsman would wish to avoid'.[50] He was reputed
to have been thanked by the police for having killed two men, probably a
school exaggeration, but nevertheless impressive. He once hit a cricket ball
over the school chapel.

At one time, Elstree had three of the best cricketers ever to be found
in one school at the same time, namely E.M.
Dowson, W.F.A. Rattigan and W.P. Robertson.
Dowson arrived aged ten and went straight into
the First XI.

Arthur T.B. Dunn* was an assistant master who
went on to found Ludgrove School. He started
with one boy in 1892, and by the time of his death
in 1902, the school list was booked to 1911.[51] He
was a great sportsman, with the unique distinction
of having been chosen for the England football
team both at left full-back and also left forward.
He was ambidextrous, and bowled almost equally

Arthur T.B. Dunn

---

* There is now an Arthur Dunn football cup for football between public schools.

Dwin Bramall,
a future Field
Marshal, in the
cricket nets

well with either hand. He was energetic, well organised, a much-respected Etonian, and founder of the Eton Mission.

One of the school's star players was Archie MacLaren (1871–1944), later captain of the England cricket team, who would go on to coach Elstree boys in the game. His father was a cotton merchant in Manchester who familiarised his son with the game, being treasurer of the Lancashire County Cricket Club. Young Archie played in Elstree's First XI for both football and cricket. He went on to Harrow, where at the age of fifteen he played in the Eton versus Harrow match, scoring top scores in both innings (fifty-five and sixty-seven) using a size-5 bat. In his last year at Harrow, he captained the first team. He distinguished himself in several Eton and Harrow matches, captaining the Harrow team in his last year and scoring seventy-six

Archie MacLaren

Masters Cricket XI, 1893

of the 133 runs on a notoriously wet day. He became 'one of the foremost figures in what is often described as the Augustan age of cricket'.[52]

In 1895, he scored 424 for Lancashire against Somerset. In 1903, he and Reggie Spooner scored 368 runs in three hours. Aged fifty-one, he scored 200 not out for the Marylebone Cricket Club (MCC) against a New Zealand XI, his last first-class innings.

At squash, the best master was Revd F. Meyrick-Jones,* described in a tribute as 'a great athlete at Marlborough, though little of a scholar'.[53] He was full of tricks – looking to the left, bringing the racquet down as if for a hard cross-shot, and then suddenly greasing it down the right side, all without turning his head.

* * * * *

There were various happenings during the time of the first Sanderson head-master. In 1875, he wrote *Zeugma: Or, Greek Steps from Primer to Author* with an assistant master, Revd F.B. Firman. In 1878, (Clinton) Edward Sowerby (1864–1900) won a scholarship to Haileybury College and went on to be a Fellow of Trinity Hall, Cambridge and a translator of Euripides.

---

* Revd Frederic Meyrick-Jones (1867–1950). In 1899, he became manager of the Rugby School Mission, a religious mission in North London.

Walter Headlam (1866–1908) was another Elstree pupil.* He went on to be one of the greatest Greek scholars of his generation, perhaps best known for *The Mimes of Herodas*. He was also a mentor to Rupert Brooke and he became a friend of Katherine Sanderson, the headmaster's wife. His brother, Cecil Headlam, went so far as to describe Lancelot Sanderson as 'one of the pioneers of the modern luxurious and efficient preparatory schools', which might not chime with the more spartan reflections of contemporary pupils. Cecil wrote of his brother: 'Here he was taught the classics and coached in cricket with equal

Walter Headlam

enthusiasm, and in due time passed on to Harrow, where he had obtained an entrance scholarship. He always retained an affection for Elstree.'[54]

In 1889, Walter himself wrote to Augustus Austen Leigh, Provost of King's College, Cambridge:

> I spent some really idyllic days at Elstree, which I love … What a pity you weren't there! It would have been the making ----! … It seems so strange to find everything so much the same, Brasier and Portsmouth (I don't believe you know who they are!) just the same. But I'm sorry poor old Gooch is dead, aren't you? And I wish the Upper 1st were still taken in the Old Study, though it makes a very nice drawing-room … I was a little disappointed that the room with the double windows where I used to sleep at 'The Elms' is no longer a dormitory.[55]

Walter Headlam was moved by a tragedy that occurred at the school when Kit Sanderson, the eldest daughter, died unexpectedly on 7 December 1887, 'in the springtime of her beautiful existence'. She was tall and slender and had long been delicate, was often in pain if she played the violin or the

---

* His brother, Arthur Francis Headlam, fourth son of Edward and Mary Headlam, died at the school on 3 July 1882.

piano, and was sometimes found crouching in pain, with tears running down her face. Her sister Agnes described her as 'a warm flame and all of us knew that warmth of that flame'.[56] The family doctor made her live quietly, but when he was replaced by a new doctor, the advice was that she ought to get out and about more and not be coddled. This was probably bad advice. In December 1887, she suddenly fell ill in agonising pain. She lay still and asked Agnes softly for a little piece of ice. She died the following morning, leaving her father 'staring in front of him with a face carved in stone'[57] and her mother comforting the bereaved family.

Kit's death inspired extensive mourning: 'All hearts were knit together in the mystery of a kindred sympathy: and on such occasions as these, silence, not words, is the best balm for the broken-hearted.'[58] The coffin, covered with white roses, eucharis, lilies of the valley and other flowers, was carried to the school chapel. After the funeral, attended by all the boys and many schoolmasters, she was buried in the chapel ground. She had been on the point of marrying the brilliant Ted (Teddy) Butler, son of the headmaster of Harrow.

Ted Butler had been a pupil at Elstree before going on to Harrow in 1880 with an Entrance Scholarship, enjoying a glittering school career. He won numerous prizes, including the Bourchier Prize for History and the Headmaster's Prize for an English essay. He was also captain of both the football and cricket teams (clinching a victory in the Eton versus Harrow match). He won the Gregory Scholarship and went on to Trinity College, Cambridge with an Exhibition. M.R. James described him as 'a magnificent being, not spoiled by his success'.[59]

Walter Headlam dedicated a threnody to her, remembered for its 'simplicity, tenderness, restraint and the beauty of a splendid epithet':

You that were
So free-hearted and so fair,
Made for life and air,
Now to lie where no man's lore
Can restore
You that were, and are no more.

Ne'er again
Death may bring such burning pain
As devoured my brain
When they told me you had died,
Ere a bride,
You so young and morning-eyed.[60]

Monty James persuaded a number of friends of Kit and Ted to subscribe for a large stained-glass window in the school chapel. The subject was the Good Shepherd, created by C.E. Kempe, and it cost £33 0s. 5d.

Other old boys who did the school proud included R.B. Benson, who won the second scholarship to Harrow in 1874, and went on to win the first scholarship to Balliol College, Oxford. James B. Richardson won the third scholarship in 1875, and went on to University College, Oxford, and then Sandhurst. He learnt Russian, joined the 5th (Royal Irish) Lancers and was killed in 1885 aged twenty-three, having gone out on 22 March in a party of three men. J.H.F. Piele won a classical scholarship to Harrow in 1877. Ted Butler himself secured a fifth equal scholarship, going to Harrow in 1880. H.H. Joachim (1868–1938) won a first-class scholarship in classics, and went on to become an Oxford logician and philosopher, Wykeham Professor of Logic, and taught T.S. Eliot. He was the author of *The Nature of Truth* (1906).

Dr Montague (Monty) Rendall (1862–1950), known as Monty, who grew to be a man of gigantic stature, won the first entrance scholarship to Harrow from Elstree in 1876. He went on to Trinity College, Cambridge with a foundation scholarship and Bell University scholarship. He later taught at Winchester from 1887, serving as headmaster between 1911 and 1924. His brother Vernon (1869–1960), a keen cricketer, went to Rugby and also won a scholarship to Trinity College, Cambridge. Rendall was an original Governor of the BBC and editor of the *Athenaeum*.

Dr Montague (Monty) Rendall

A pupil of a different kind was George Bullough, later Sir George Bullough, 1st Bt (1870–1939), a playboy famed for his thoroughbred race-horses. He came from a Lancashire family and inherited a half-interest in Howard & Bullough, his father's textile business. His brother Ian was married to Lily Elsie between 1911 and 1930. Bullough built Kinloch Castle on the Isle of Rùm (or Rhum). His main interests were yachting and horse racing. He used his steam-powered yacht, *Rhouma*, as a hospital ship in the Second Boer War, and sailed it to South Africa for service. For this, he was knighted by Edward VII. In the First World War, he became a superintendent with the Remount Department, and in 1916 was created a baronet. As a racehorse owner, he was a member of the Jockey Club and won the 1917 War National, the Gold Cup at Ascot and the Eclipse Stakes, and later the 1,000 Guineas. He died while playing golf in France in 1939.

* * * * *

There was a great increase in pupils during Revd Sanderson's time. He began with forty-seven pupils in 1869, and soon had fifty new boys each year. To accommodate boys and staff, the headmaster bought several houses. This led to variable standards of living, with one boy sleeping on a mattress in an attic. The aforementioned Monty Rendall, one of his most distinguished pupils, noted that Revd Sanderson was 'the presiding and animating genius of Elstree' with the 'clear-cut intellectual features and the air of dignity and refinement which his presence suggested'.[61] Sanderson also bought about 300 acres of land. As mentioned, he built a swimming pool, squash courts, and levelled the lawn tennis courts.

In 1870, Lancelot Sanderson erected a temporary chapel, before commissioning Sir Arthur Blomfield to build a new chapel that could seat 250 people and be the glory of Elstree. It was built of dark red brick and red Dumfries stone. The foundation stone was laid by Dr Butler in 1876 and it was consecrated in 1877. Parents and old boys presented an organ costing £320.

Sadly, nothing remains of this chapel, which played such a significant part in the life of the school. The intention had been to retain it when the Oliver Borthwick Memorial Trust bought Elstree Hill school premises, but no congregation could be found. Vandals attacked it and the fittings were eventually sold. Finally, in 1956, it was pulled down. The three coffins buried there and the six boxes of ashes were moved to Elstree Parish Church.

* * * * *

There was a fire brigade at Elstree composed of members of Revd Sanderson's household, run by its captain, T. Brazier, the school's butler. He invented a canvas chute attached to two stout ropes, which formed stays for wooden rungs. This could be packed away into a small space, but could be brought out at a moment's notice and attached to a window. When first introduced, it was attached to a third-storey window at the school, and after two or three members of the brigade tested it, Revd Lancelot Sanderson, Revd Vernon Royle, C.P. Wilson, Fred MacDonnell and Arthur Dunn all went down it, followed by a great many boys. It was still in use in 1939, judged effective by Commander Sanderson, though firemen disapproved of it because a person had once gone down it with a nail in his shoe, tearing a hole in the canvas, through which the next man down fell. Wilson, MacDonnell and Dunn sang very well and would entertain the Sanderson family and the boys with classical and light glees.

C.P. Wilson left Elstree in 1898, along with W.P. (Will) Hornby. Together, they founded Sandroyd School, converting a tutorial establishment into a modern preparatory school.

* * * * *

In 1878, tragedy struck when Robert Blair Montgomery Birch, the only surviving son of Lieutenant Colonel F.M. Birch, died at the school, aged twelve.

In 1881, the school was the site of a match between MCC and Elstree. On 8 April 1885, Revd Vernon Royle,[*] then a master at the school, married Eleanor Agnes Sanderson, daughter of John Sanderson and therefore a niece of Revd Lancelot Sanderson.

---

[*] Revd V. Royle played cricket for Lancashire. It was debatable whether he or Johnny Briggs were the better fielder at cover point. He was renowned for having thrown down Ephraim Lockwood's wicket, and for disposing of him 'by one of the most wonderful catches ever seen' a few years before.

In September 1887, Lord and Lady Randolph Churchill sent their younger son Jack to the school. He was a bit homesick at first, and sent affectionate letters to his mother: 'Do you miss me much? I do you. I hope Papa is quite well give him my love and a million kisses.'[62] Jack was visited regularly at the school by his mother and the beloved family nanny, Mrs Everest, with whom he would walk around the school. The autumn of 1888 coincided with the famous Jack the Ripper murders, as a result of which Jack took to signing himself to his parents: 'Jack, not the Ripper'.[63]

Occasionally, his brother Winston would come over to see Jack from Harrow. Jack told him to go in at the front door and ask for Mrs Sanderson. They would then dine alone with her so that the other boys did not know.[64]

Despite a bad eye, Jack did well at Elstree, coming top of every class and comparing well with Winston's efforts at Harrow. During his years there, however, Elstree suffered from epidemics of measles, mumps, whooping cough, chicken pox, influenza, ringworm and eye infections. Jack was about to see an important cricket match at Lord's, a treat arranged by Mr Sanderson, when he went down with mumps, thereby missing the match. His mother bought him a pony as a consolation.

Dr Welldon kept a place for Jack at Harrow in May 1892, and examined him that July. He passed on his first attempt. Thus, in September 1892, he joined Winston there, and became the youngest boy at the school, entering a year early at twelve and a half.*

Another Elstree boy, A. Stafford Crawley (1876–1948), who was there in 1887, went on to become a Canon of St George's Chapel, Windsor. St John Hutchinson (1884–1942), the barrister and Liberal MP, arrived in 1894.

The masters also did the school proud, many of them setting up schools of their own. Most notable was Arthur Dunn, who, as mentioned previously, taught at Elstree from 1885 to 1892. He had previously tutored a family in Ireland. He was a proficient footballer and cricketer. In May 1892, he opened his own school, Ludgrove, then at Monken Hadley, near Barnet. Sadly, he died in his sleep at the age of forty-one, in February 1902.

---

* Jack Churchill went into the City, becoming a partner in stockbrokers Vickers, da Costa in 1918. He married Lady Gwendeline Bertie. Their daughter, Clarissa (1920–2021), married Anthony Eden, later Earl of Avon, KG.

Ludgrove moved to its present site at Wixenford, near Wokingham, in 1937, and has thus remained within match-playing distance of Elstree.

* * * * *

By 1896, Lancelot Sanderson was physically worn out. His health had deteriorated sharply after the death of his daughter, and he suffered from attacks of faintness. Only at the time of his death was it publicly revealed that for twenty years he had been subject to epileptic fits, while 'his intense enthusiasm for work kept him at his post.'*[65] Some felt he stayed on too long. A partnership was created between him, his son Ted, and Revd Vernon Royle, the latter two acquiring an eighth interest in the school.

Matters continued to deteriorate. Ted Sanderson, who had been teaching at Elstree since 1893, set off to the South African War and, as we shall see, remained there for health reasons until 1911. The next headmaster then decided to move into the School House and thought that Revd Sanderson should move out, which he refused to do.

By 1900, Revd Sanderson was living in a dreary house called Placilla on Lansdowne Road in Worthing, hoping in vain to return to Elstree. He never did. He continued to take an interest in the school, not least in the rabbits that overran the school grounds. To his son Philip he wrote, urging him to work hard, to 'put a *strong* & patient hand sickle into the harvest which is coming so close to you', and telling him that if he did not waver, he should get 'a valuable scholarship and a First Class'.[66]

He died in Worthing on 10 December 1904. He was praised in *The Times* for having worked the school 'up to a high position among the preparatory schools of the kingdom', and it was stated that it was 'largely through his whole-hearted enthusiasm both for work and play that the school gained its reputation not only for scholarships, but also as the forcing ground of some of the finest cricketers of the day.'[67]

A memorial service was held in the school chapel, and soon afterwards a fund was raised in his memory with the idea of installing a clock there.

---

* Sylvia Townsend Warner gave a lurid fictional account of him frequently lying on the floor, as family and staff stepped over him.

The clock was presented in 1906 and chimed the Westminster chime every quarter of an hour.

Mrs Kitty, his widow, continued to live in Worthing with two of her daughters until 1921. All the family money had been ploughed into the school, including the building of the chapel, and so there was little left for her. Sadly, after her death, many boxes of her letters were thrown away and her books were sold, including a complete set of Conrads, signed and dedicated to her. Her son Philip hastened home from Bombay when he heard she was ill, arriving after she died. Thankfully, he was able to rescue a few Conrads.[*]

The old chapel at Elstree

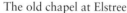

---

[*] The rescued books included a copy of *Almayer's Folly* (1895) with the inscription 'To Mrs Katherine S.O. Sanderson from her affectionate and obedient servant the author Conrad Natycz Korzeniowski'; *The Nigger of the Narcissus* with 'To dear Mrs Sanderson from her affectionate and obedient servant the Author, 1st Dec 1897'; *Typhoon* with 'To Mrs Sanderson with unalterable regard, affection and gratitude, from her most faithful and obedient servant the Author, 1903'; and *The Mirror of the Sea*, which was dedicated to her thus: 'To Dear Mrs Sanderson this copy of a work honoured by the imprint of her name from her affectionate friend and very obedient servant the Author, 4 Oct 1906 Pent Farm [at Postling, near Hythe]'.

CHAPTER SIX

REVD VERNON ROYLE
(1854–1929)

HEADMASTER 1900

Revd Vernon Peter Royle (1854–1929) was only headmaster at Elstree very briefly, though he had been a respected assistant master since 1879. He fell out with Lancelot Sanderson, his wife's uncle, when Sanderson refused to retire formally and leave School House. Thereupon Royle gave a term's notice, and leased a large mansion called Stanmore Park, in Middlesex, a mere four miles away. He founded his own school there, which he opened in January 1901, taking three Elstree masters with him (including William Nichols Roe, a well-known cricketing and mathematics master)

Revd Vernon Royle

and eighty boys. Elstree was left with just twenty-five pupils, its lowest moment. Whatever Elstree may have thought of this defection at the time, there is no doubt Royle was a remarkable figure, *The Times* describing him as 'one of the most famous cover-points that cricket has ever produced.'[68]

Royle had been born at Brooklands, Cheshire in 1854, played cricket in the First XI at Rossall School, and then went up to Brasenose College, Oxford. He played first-class cricket for Lancashire in 1873, scoring 1,423 runs, with an average of 16.31. He was a brilliant fielder at cover point, doing especially well for Oxford in 1876. He went to Australia with Lord Harris's team in 1878–9 and made five catches at cover point in a match with Victoria in Melbourne. Altogether, he played 102 first-class matches before 1891 (including seventy-four for Lancashire and one during the Test match in Australia). He was also a good footballer.

He was also noted as a fast run-getter, hitting the ball with power, and having started as a fast bowler, he later developed a talent for slow bowling. It helped that he was ambidextrous and very quick on his feet. He was a master at judging the short run and kept his fielding secrets to himself. F.B. Wilson said he was 'not the player to give the geese a warning that there was a fox prowling about'.[69]

He was credited with encouraging many a young cricketer to glories on the pitch at Elstree, including his brother-in-law, John Tunstall Sanderson, at Elstree, who played in a memorable Eton versus Harrow match at Lord's in 1885, captained by Ted Butler for Harrow, and the future Marquess of Willingdon for Eton.

Royle was ordained in 1881 and was also curate of Aldenham, Watford while at the school. He was known affectionately as Johnny, and one pupil paid him the slightly odd tribute: 'Johnny rarely ever caned the wrong boy.'[70] Sir Lancelot Sanderson (1863–1944) commended his 'wonderful influence' both at Elstree and later at Stanmore, concluding: 'It is good to think that his influence will be felt through many generations of men who are now and who will be in the future playing their part in the world.'[71]

When he taught French, he had a particular method of explaining the difference between the grave and acute accent in which he imitated his own French teacher: 'Ah! The grave he come slow from left to right, so, coming slowly over the boy's head, and the acute he come smart from right to left: So! Clipping him on the ear. Now you not forget him, eh?'[72]

He was crippled with rheumatism in later life, and walked with two sticks. He died in May 1929. On the day of his funeral, which was attended by a number of Sandersons (including Elstree's headmaster Ted), flags at Lord's cricket ground were lowered to half-mast, while the boys at Stanmore played a cricket match.

In 1938, Stanmore Park Preparatory School merged with another school in Hertfordshire, and the building was demolished the same year.

The South African War

The South African War took place during this period. One of those who sailed to take part in the action was Ted Sanderson, in the teeth of opposition from Conrad, who made it clear to him that he thought the war was pointless and that Russia was more of a threat to England. Ted was one of those that survived. The war (which is sometimes referred to as the Second Boer War) claimed nine old boys of the school and, in hindsight, was a forerunner to the terrible loss of young men's lives in the Great War of 1914–18.

Amongst those who died in South Africa was Trooper George Lamb, from Devon, who served with the Bechuanaland Border Police. He was killed in action in the Jameson Raid at Krugersdorp on 1 February 1896. Lieutenant Colonel Claude Sitwell, DSO, a cousin of Sir George Sitwell (father of Osbert, Edith and Sacheverell) fell at Hart's Hill in 1900. He had good knowledge of Arabic and led the Sudanese troops who formed Uganda's garrison. He was often on remote, undeveloped frontier posts, frequently travelling from Kampala on foot, and once plunged through bad swamps up to his shoulders. He inspired trust in his men, and after a mutiny amongst Sudanese troops in 1897, his was the only company not disarmed. In July 1898, he was one of the first Europeans to ascend to the snows of the Rwenzori Mountains (first discovered by the explorer Henry Morton Stanley in 1889). He travelled to South Africa in 1899 with the Royal Dublin Fusiliers to fight, only to be killed in action.

Lieutenant James Gething, of the South Wales Borderers, died in 1901 from injuries sustained falling off his horse on 3 July 1901, while Lieutenant J.S. Watney, on the staff of the Middlesex Yeomanry, was killed leading a charge at Tweefontein on Christmas Day 1901, aged just eighteen. Lieutenant Roland Buxton, 2nd Battalion, Norfolk Regiment (Mounted Regiment) served in West Africa on the Niger from 1897 to 1898, was mentioned in dispatches in 1899, and was then employed with the West African Frontier Force. He was killed near Sterkfontein on 13 December 1901.[73] Captain Edgar Mark-Wardlaw, Adjutant of the Duke of Cornwall's Light Infantry, whose grandfather had served with Nelson on the *Victory*, fell on 18 February 1900.

Lieutenant Richard Hobson, from Cheshire, was a keen shot at school and won the Spencer Cup at Bisley in 1895 with the highest possible score. He served with the King's Royal Rifle Corps from 1898 and was killed at the engagement at Schippen's Farm on 5 June 1900. Lieutenant Robert Kinnear, from New South Wales, Australia, joined the 5th Dragoon Guards in 1899, and died in South Africa on 16 March 1900. Finally, there is a window in Melton Mowbray dedicated to Captain Gordon Wood, who commanded the Shropshire Company of the Imperial Yeomanry. He was killed in action near Zeerust on 20 October 1900.

The South African War was considered such a tragedy that a host of Elstree old boys attended the unveiling of an alabaster memorial plaque in the school chapel. It was unveiled by Major General W.H. Mackinnon on 11 July 1904, with Dr Butler of Harrow addressing pupils past and present and the relatives of those who had died. The plaque is now to be found in the Bramall Sports Hall.

CHAPTER SEVEN

REVD EDGAR STOGDON
(1870–1951)

HEADMASTER 1901–3

With the departure of Revd Royle, the school was at its lowest ebb. Ted Sanderson was still in Africa so could do little to help, but he was able to appoint another distinguished cricketer to become the new headmaster.

Edgar Stogdon (1870–1951) had been born at Harrow on 30 July 1870, and was both an entrance and leaving scholar. He went up to Clare College, Cambridge. He was known as a right-hand batsman, played cricket twice for Cambridge,[*] represented the university twice against Oxford in the mile race, and played football for Arsenal in 1890.

Stogdon became a vicar in 1895, taught classics at Uppingham and served as their school chaplain. At Elstree, he took charge of the teaching side of life, while Mrs Kitty Sanderson ran the domestic side, the finances and dealt with correspondence.

There were numerous financial difficulties when he took over, which were partly resolved by selling off all but twenty-six of the 300 acres that Lancelot Sanderson had acquired over the years.

Stogdon would not be at the school for long, however. Seven new boys arrived in 1901, thirteen in 1902, and fifteen in 1903. Following these trying years, Stogdon left to become an assistant master at Harrow early in 1903, by which time Elstree only had twenty-four boys. Whilst at Harrow, he helped set up the School Volunteer Corps and then left to take charge of the Harrow Mission in 1908. In 1914, he married Louise Dundas, who died in 1940. He returned to Harrow as Vicar of Aldenham from 1923 to 1944,

---

[*] His brother, John Stogdon, played forty-four first-class matches for MCC.

then as Vicar and Rural Dean of Harrow, and remained devoted to Harrow for the rest of his life.

He sounds an endearing character. He once wrote to *The Times* to point out that Harrovians were embarrassed to be seen walking with ladies in the streets at school. They instructed their mothers as to which hat to wear, and would try to put her off if her figure was beyond 'the accepted standard'. He continued: 'Mr Winston Churchill invited his old nurse down for a day at Harrow to her intense happiness; she arrived in an old poke bonnet, her figure had attained ample proportions, and Mr Churchill walked arm-in-arm with her in the streets. It is about the nicest thing a Harrow boy has ever done.'[74]

He promoted the idea that Eton and Harrow were 'mortal enemies but immortal friends'.[75] Along with Dr Cyril Norwood, Harrow's celebrated headmaster, Stogdon believed the school gave its pupils a sense of initiative and responsibility. It became an accepted part of Founder's Day that he would kick off the match informally.

He died in Northwood on 30 June 1951.

CHAPTER EIGHT

REVD FRANKLYN DE WINTON LUSHINGTON (1868–1941)

HEADMASTER 1903–11

Revd Franklyn de Winton Lushington (1868–1941) was born in Madras on 29 March 1868, where his father, Sir Franklyn Lushington, was Accountant General. The Lushingtons were an established landed gentry family from Kent. One of his distant cousins was Kitty Maxse, on whom Virginia Woolf based her character Mrs Dalloway. Lushington was educated at Clare College, Cambridge, and then became an assistant master at Elstree from 1892 to 1899. He was also assistant curate at St James's Church in Bury St Edmunds.

He was a great admirer of Revd Lancelot Sanderson, of whom he wrote with 'sincere affection and respect' and whom he described as 'endeared to me and to many by acts of great personal kindness'.[76] In his book of sermons, he addressed the boys with less ferocity than Revd Bernays, but

Revd Franklyn de
Winton Lushington

was keen on admonishing the boys 'to whom the greater temptations and responsibilities of public-life are entirely unknown'.[77] He firmly believed that there was a greater opportunity to shape and direct the characters of boys at prep school when their minds were 'more open to impressions from without' and their faith 'still unclouded' by their troubles or sins. He also maintained that the character of a school depended on the moral tone of the young boys, since it was with them that the new boys first associated and from whom they absorbed the example of standards of behaviour and principles. In his sermons, he intended to instil the 'right impressions' and 'a sense of their own individual responsibility'.[78]

Lushington drew the attention of the boys to contemporary events in order to make his points – the memorial to Lord Lawrence in Westminster Abbey, and the sudden death from a heart attack of the Archbishop of Canterbury, Edward Benson, while he was attending Sunday service at St Deiniol's Church, Hawarden, Wales (whilst staying with then prime minister, W.E. Gladstone). He told the boys that Dr Vaughan had asked for no memoir or permanent record of his life to be written: 'I desire no other memorial than the kind thoughts of my former pupils.'[79] Without presumably knowing the reason for this, he asked the boys: 'Do you not think that they are words which each one of us would like to be able to say, when for us too, the night of this our mortal life is far spent, and the day is close at hand when we shall rise to the life immortal with Christ in God?'[80]

The murder of the actor William Terriss (father of Ellaline Terriss) by a deranged actor on 16 December 1897 was worked into a sermon, as was the Diamond Jubilee of Queen Victoria in 1897 and her death in 1901. Inevitably, Lushington's words sound stern to modern ears, as he spoke loftily to his young flock. He told leaving boys that he was sure that many would have 'memories of many very happy days spent here – memories of days when you resisted some temptation, of days when you tried to work your best or play your best.' But then he turned to the inevitable bad memories too:

> Try to find out what it was that was wrong or weak in you; and then, when you have found it out, pray to God to forgive you for it. And then this bad

memory will not be there to haunt you, and to make you fear for the future, because it reminds you of your weakness in the past; but it will be there to warn you, and out of your very weakness God will make you strong.

It is no good trying to cover up the bad memories. That is what the poor man does when he takes to drink, in order that he may forget his poverty, and so becomes poorer than before. Money can remove very many of the discomforts of life. There is one thing which it can never do for us: it cannot give us the power to forget.[81]

Not everyone would have agreed with Lushington that when men were killed as they were in the war on the Indian frontier, they were 'dying as a soldier would wish to die, on the field of battle.'[82]

He cemented his relationship with the school in 1899 by marrying Monica Sydney Sanderson (1872–1934), who had inspired John Galsworthy so vividly at the outset of his burgeoning literary career. After their marriage, they went to St Paul's Pro-Cathedral in Valletta in 1901, from where he would become Archdeacon of Malta from 1902 to 1903. Lushington then served as headmaster of Elstree between 1903 and 1911.

One of his early ideas was to form an alliance with Mr W.A. Rolles Biddle's preparatory school in Kensington, from which a number of boys came to Elstree over the years. He then took Revd George Scott into partnership. To begin with, he had only two masters, T.C. Weatherhead, a fine scholar and Corinthian footballer, and W.G. Byron-Harker, who stayed until 1934. The latter was a quiet man who did not play games due to a tram accident in early life. He was dormitory master and specialised in helping the more backward boys pass the Common Entrance exam. Ian Sanderson thought especially well of him.

The school days were long. The top form worked for an hour before breakfast and their prep period ended at 8.15 p.m. The juniors did not have early school, and the very youngest went to bed at 7.30 p.m. The boys still wore Eton jackets and black silk top hats on Sundays in 1910. In winter, they wore grey tweed knickerbockers; in summer, they wore grey flannel suits with long trousers. There were no half-terms, only an exeat for the Eton and Harrow match, but occasionally they were allowed out to tea.

Punishment was drill in the yard, and if a boy had four drills in one week, he was beaten on Saturday morning.

On 11 November 1909, Richard Handcock died at the school after a thirty-six-hour illness of meningitis. His parents presented the school chapel with a window in his memory and it was dedicated by the Bishop of London in 1910.

There were many old boys from this period who rose to distinction. Sir Harcourt Gold (1876–1952) followed a distinguished rowing career by becoming a coach, leading the famous Leander crew to beat the Belgians in the Olympic Regatta at Henley in 1908. He was knighted for services to rowing. Sir Alan Anderson (1877–1952), son of the pioneering physician and suffragette Dr Elizabeth Garrett Anderson, a keen oarsman, went on to be Controller of Railways at the Ministry of War Transport and chairman of the Railway Executive. In 1917, he accompanied A.J. Balfour to Washington and helped set up control of wheat in America and Canada. Shipping was his first love, however, and he was commended as 'one of those who all too rarely enlighten our lives with an armoury full of endearing gifts'.[83] Air Vice-Marshal Sir Oliver Swann (1878–1948) was a pioneer of naval aviation. Lord Lyle of Westbourne (1882–1954) was a member of the Lyle family (part of the Tate & Lyle dynasty), and nicknamed 'Mr Cube', with his portrait on every packet of sugar sold by the company. Sir Philip Joubert (1887–1965) became a distinguished air commander, overseeing RAF Coastal Command during the war. His obituary described him as a man 'never hampered by the cares of the introvert'.[84] He was well known to the public for the many broadcasts he gave during the Second World War. Major Bevil Rudd (1894–1948), a noted athlete, founded the Achilles Club, which brought university athletes into open competition and which restarted Anglo-American inter-university challenges. Sir Cecil Ames (1897–1977) was at the school from 1907 to 1911. He went on to Dover College, later becoming a solicitor, joining the Nigerian Administrative Service, and rising to be Puisne Judge at the Supreme Court there. He then went on to serve at the Court of Appeal in the Gambia and Sierra Leone.

Bertram Mills, famous for his circus, sent both his sons to the school. Cyril Mills (1902–1991) would go on to work as a spook for MI6, and was particularly active during the Second World War. After their father's death in 1938, he and his brother ran the circus until it closed in 1967. Bernard Mills (1905–1985) was a notable horseman and took charge of the animal acts and trainers.

It was while Lushington was headmaster that a subway was constructed under the road due to the dangers of increased traffic. It cost £300.

* * * * *

In 1911, Lushington was invited to become headmaster of Dover College, where Galsworthy was an occasional visitor. He remained there until heading off on active service in the First World War.

In later life, he enjoyed lecturing on literary subjects in Britain and the USA, speaking on poetry and education. In 1931, he was Vicar of King's Langley and preached to the boys in the school chapel in the Michaelmas term. He lived at St Barnabas, Lingfield, Surrey and 2 Whitehall Court. He died in London on 30 March 1941, and was survived by their only daughter, Evelyn Monica, born in 1906, who married Roger Wimbush.

CHAPTER NINE

E.L. SANDERSON
(1867–1939)

HEADMASTER 1911–35

E.L. Sanderson (1867–1939), better known to us as Ted, took over as headmaster in 1911. We have already met the young Ted. He had an extraordinarily rich intellectual background, and was noted for his close friendships with John Galsworthy and Joseph Conrad. He himself had been a pupil at Elstree

E.L. Sanderson and Helen Mary Sanderson

before going on to Harrow, where he shone, and King's College, Cambridge. His sister Agnes admired him hugely for his keen scholarship, his athleticism and his eyes 'deep blue as only to be found in the sea'.[85] As the oldest in a huge family, he was naturally authoritative from an early age.

Ted was an assistant master at Elstree for six years until 1900, when he sailed with the 3rd Battalion, Yorkshire Volunteers to serve in the South African War. Already sickly, his health was further seriously damaged, and he did not return to England until 1911. From 1904 until his return, he had a government appointment as town clerk in the Transvaal Education Department. During his time in Africa, his wife Helen contributed perceptive African sketches to *Scribner's Magazine* under the name of Janet Allardyce.

While out there, their daughter Katharine (Kit) married Charles MacGregor Taylor, a pioneer coffee planter who had arrived in 1908. He

E.L. Sanderson
and Staff, 1911

had a wife who had been a Gaiety Girl, but he divorced her to marry Kit. He was one of the founders of the famous Muthaiga Country Club in Nairobi, and bought land next to the farm of Elspeth Huxley's parents. It is thought that the love affair with Kit found its way into Huxley's famous book *The Flame Trees of Thika* (1959). Kit was well known for charity work with children and lived to be 100.* When at last Ted returned to Britain, he took over as headmaster from his brother-in-law, Revd F. de W. Lushington.

Conrad rejoiced with Ted's sister Agnes Ridgeway in June 1911 that Ted was 'in England', in his 'rightful place' as headmaster and, moreover, 'making a success from the very beginning'. He congratulated Ted on the 'effective use' of his influence in high places, welcoming his appointment as headmaster:

> I rejoiced exceedingly at you taking up this work for which your hardly
> acquired experience of men and things makes you even more fit than you
> were before! I don't forget the material improvement which has its great

---

* Katharine Graham Sanderson (1899–1999) lived to attend the 150th anniversary of the school. Her daughter, Kathini Graham (1929–2012), was working for Sir Philip Mitchell, then Governor of Kenya, during Princess Elizabeth's visit in 1952, during which she became Queen Elizabeth II. Kathini was responsible for organising a black hat to be delivered to the plane so that the new queen could wear it when she descended the plane steps.

importance; but my most affectionate wishes go to the guardian of the best sort of learning and of the best traditions, taking up the care of young minds in this troubled time of disappearing landmarks.[86]

The First World War

Not long after Ted took over, Britain went to war with Germany in what was then called the Great War. A great number of former Elstree pupils of varying ages died during those years.

The school did not have a large roster, but it suffered many wartime losses. This was a devastating time for British prep schools and public schools. In 1915, for instance, Winchester did not send a single pupil to Oxford or Cambridge for the first and only time in its 600-year history, as over 90 per cent of boys leaving that year went and enlisted straight away. One Wykehamist is mentioned on the Elstree roll. Nearly thirty Elstree boys were killed near Ypres, several dying within days of each other. The effect that the knowledge of these losses would have had on a small community such as Elstree is best highlighted by the numbers of brothers who lost their lives, with six pairs of brothers listed on the memorial.

In one poignant case, one brother died in the First World War and his brother lived on to die in the Second World War: R.C. Blagrove, adjutant of the 6th Battalion, The Duke of Cornwall's Light Infantry, died on 12 August 1915; his brother, Rear Admiral Henry Blagrove, became the first senior British naval officer to die in the Second World War, on 14 October 1939, soon after his appointment as Commander of the 2nd Battleship Squadron of the Home Fleet, when HMS *Royal Oak* was hit by a German U-47 submarine.

The names of all who died are commemorated on a handsome plaque inside the front door of the school at Woolhampton. Today they are just a list, and inevitably many of the names will not be familiar to current pupils and staff. But behind these names lie tragic stories, as the cream of Britain's youth were wiped out in large numbers.

It would be possible to tell the story of many gallant soldiers, but possibly the most poignant way of making the point is to observe this photograph of the cricket XI in 1910, a group of confident boys on the brink of life, and to realise that six of these pupils lost their lives whilst serving their country in wartime.

Cricket XI of which six were killed in the war

The six who died were as follows (starting from the back row and moving from left to right):

2nd Lieutenant Arthur Cyril Lawson (1896–1917) was the only son of Arthur Ernest Lawson, CIE. He was born in Madras and went on to Wellington and the School of Mines, Camborne. In 1914, he joined the Artists' Rifles, and was transferred to the Rifle Brigade as 2nd Lieutenant, 7th Battalion. He served with the British Expeditionary Force in France and Flanders from August 1915. He was wounded at Arras in March 1916 and died in No.4 London General Hospital on 6 July 1917. He is buried in the Brompton Cemetery.

2nd Lieutenant John Bell Hughes (1898–1917) was the eldest son of Major O.J. Bell, 13th Welsh Fusiliers, and adopted son of John Hughes, of The Manor House, Hampton-on-Thames. After Harrow, he joined the 6th Middlesex Regiment as a private, drilling recruits and was gazetted 2nd

65

Lieutenant. He was sent to France on 20 August 1917, attached to the 2/5 Battalion Lancashire Fusiliers. He went over in the attack of 20 September 1917 and was very soon killed. He was buried on the battlefield, near a spot called Schuler Galeries, about three miles south-east of Pilkem.

2nd Lieutenant John Christopher Frederick Magnay (1896–1917), son of Frederick William Magnay, of Drayton, Norfolk. He went on to Harrow, and was gazetted 2nd Lieutenant, 1st Battalion, Norfolk Regiment in December 1914. He was killed in action at Vimy Ridge on 23 April 1917, ten days after his cousin, Lieutenant Colonel Philip Magnay, also died there. He is commemorated on the Arras Memorial, bay 3.

2nd Lieutenant Lionel St George Mordaunt-Smith (1896–1915), son of Mordaunt Mordaunt-Smith, of Milton Bank, Laugharne, Carmarthenshire. He attended Charterhouse and the Royal Military Academy, Sandhurst. He was gazetted 2nd Lieutenant, Royal Inniskilling Fusiliers in October 1914. He joined his battalion in the trenches three weeks later, and remained there until he was killed gallantly leading his platoon against the German trenches during the Second Battle of Ypres at Richebourg-Saint Vaast, Pas de Calais, France on 15 May 1915.

Cadet Guy Deane Thorley (1900–1918) was the youngest son of Joseph Thorley, of Wood Hall, Shenley, Hertfordshire. He became a cadet in the Bedfordshire Regiment, attached to 19th O.C. Battalion. He died on 3 August 1918 in the Military War Hospital, Napsbury, St Albans. His brother, Horace William Thorley, Lieutenant 17th Lancers, was killed in action on 8 August 1918, aged twenty-three.

Lieutenant Cyril Arthur George Lutyens (1897–1917) was the youngest son of Arthur Anstruther Lutyens. He was educated at Harrow, where he played in the cricket XI. He received his Commission in the Coldstream Guards in January 1916, went to France on 17 July that year, and was gazetted as lieutenant three days later. He was in command of his company in the attack on Houthoulst Wood, Passchendaele on 9 October 1917. After gaining his objective, he was killed by a shell which burst in his company headquarters. He is commemorated on the Tyne Cot Memorial. His adjutant wrote: 'I shall never forget Cyril coming into Battalion H.Q. (a shell hole) to ask for orders about his left flank. He came up and saluted in the middle of a very heavy shelling, as if he were on parade, and cheered us all up by joking about a cut he had got on his hand — that was the last I saw of him.'

Five of the team survived, amongst them Cyril Lutyens's older brother, Francis Murray Bernard Lutyens, MC (1895–1954), who is seated on the left. Francis served as a lieutenant in the Coldstream Guards from 1914 to 1922, and was awarded the Military Cross in 1918 for conspicuous gallantry and devotion to duty. During a particular attack, he showed a great disregard for personal danger and was a continual inspiration to his men. He led his own company and rallied the remnants of a neighbouring company, organising the captured objective for defence under heavy shell and machine gun fire. It was due to his dispositions that several counter-attacks were destroyed.

The Lutyens brothers also had a cousin who was killed during the war. Lieutenant (Lionel F.) Derek Lutyens (1894–1918), 10th Battalion, Royal Fusiliers, went to France with his regiment in 1915, and remained there as a bombing officer until after the battles of Pozieres and La Boisselle. He transferred to the General List around November 1916, and to the Royal Flying Corps on 29 March 1917. He completed three years of training, two months at the aerial gunnery in Oxford, and eight months experimental flying in all types of aircraft. He was killed on active service during a test flight in Surrey on 8 May 1918, when pressure tests on his tailplane failed. He was buried at Thursley, alongside three generations of the Lutyens family, the gravestone the work of his uncle, Sir Edwin Lutyens, who lost five nephews in the First World War. Sir Edwin went on to design the headstones for the Commonwealth War Graves.

The other survivors from the photograph were R. Findlay, L.H. Mackay and, seated at the front, W.O. Butler and J.A. Barton.

None of the victims was mourned so widely or memorably as Major Robert Gregory, MC (1881–1918). It is hard not to think of him as one of the great losses of the First World War. It is equally hard to know which of his many talents to hail as supreme. He played cricket for Ireland, taking eight for eighty with leg spin bowling in a first-class match against Scotland in 1912 (this would be the fourth-best match for Ireland, and his bowling average of 10.22 was Ireland's second-best record). He excelled at bowls (playing Ireland's tenth-best match); he boxed (a lightweight boxer against Cambridge) and was a fine equestrian, both in the hunting field and racing point-to-point.

Major Robert Gregory, MC

Gregory was born in County Galway on 20 May 1881, the only child of Rt Hon. Sir William Gregory, KCMG, of Coole Park, Gort, County Galway, formerly an MP and Governor of Ceylon (who died in March 1892, when Robert was eleven), and of the famous Lady Gregory. Lady Gregory had founded the Irish Literary Theatre and the Dublin's Abbey Theatre, and had been an inspiration for the poet W.B. Yeats. One of his Elstree masters, A.J. Richardson,* wrote: 'He had, as a boy, an affectionate nature and a penetrating mind, and seemed to me to be one of the ablest boys I ever had under me.'[87] Robert went from Elstree to Harrow, was an entrance scholar to New College, Oxford, and then studied under Henry Tonks at the Slade School of Art between 1903 and 1905.

In 1908, he staged *Deirdre*, a Yeats play, in London, starring Mrs Patrick Campbell, having originally designed the sets at the Abbey Theatre. He was also an accomplished artist, working in the studio of the French belle époque artist Jacques Émile Blanche, who wrote that he had reached 'the highest level of artistic and intellectual merit.' His paintings were exhibited alongside the work of Augustus John and William Orpen at the Chenil Gallery in London in 1914. Augustus John was best man at his wedding when he married Margaret Graham-Parry in 1907.

He joined the war effort in 1915, first with the 4th Connaught Rangers, and later in the Royal Flying Corps. He was appointed Chevalier of

---

* Arthur J. Richardson (1864–1941), known as 'Squasher', left Elstree in 1898 to found St Peter's Court, Broadstairs where, partly because he was a friend of the royal tutor, Henry Hansell, he later tutored Prince Henry, Duke of Gloucester, and Prince George, Duke of Kent.

the Légion d'Honneur and awarded the Military Cross for conspicuous gallantry and devotion to duty.

He was accidentally killed on 23 January 1918, when an Italian pilot shot his plane down by mistake as he flew back from across Austrian lines. His colonel wrote of him: 'His work was from the first invariably magnificent, his skill and courage were superlative, and he always did more than was asked of him, if possible.' To which his flight-commander added: 'He was a really fine airman and a dead game man, always out to do as much work as anyone else, and a little more, and, though officially not supposed to go over the lines, he came with us nearly every day.'

Clearly a man of great achievement, it has been suggested that he was talented but lazy, more interested in sport than academe. During the war, he became one of the most experienced pilots in the Royal Flying Corps and told George Bernard Shaw that this was the most satisfactory period in his life because of the intensity.

After his death, W.B. Yeats, his mother's great friend, wrote four poems eulogizing him. It is on account of the third poem, 'An Irish Airman Foresees His Death' (1919), that he is best remembered today:[*]

> I know that I shall meet my fate
> Somewhere among the clouds above;
> Those that I fight I do not hate
> Those that I guard I do not love;
> My country is Kiltartan Cross,
> My countrymen Kiltartan's poor,
> No likely end could bring them loss
> Or leave them happier than before.
> Nor law, nor duty bade me fight,
> Nor public man, nor cheering crowds,
> A lonely impulse of delight
> Drove to this tumult in the clouds;
> I balanced all, brought all to mind,

---

[*] The other poems were 'In Memory of Major Robert Gregory', 'Shepherd and Goatherd', and 'Reprisals'.

The years to come seemed waste of breath,
A waste of breath the years behind
In balance with this life, this death.

His death also affected George Bernard Shaw, who wrote to his mother: 'To a man with his power of standing up to danger – which must mean enjoying it – war must have intensified his life as nothing else could; he got a grip of it that he could not through art or love. I suppose that is what makes the soldier.'[88]

Many years later, in 1940, Michael Aldous, later a GP (1934–2017), arrived at the school aged six. He was very homesick during his early days and was allowed to share a room with Sandy Sanderson, son of the headmaster. The Commander used to come in each morning and give him chocolate biscuits to stop his tears. He was at the school when the Second World War ended. In May 1945, the school danced around a bonfire and burnt an effigy of Hitler. Aldous went on to become head boy, and so it fell to him on Armistice Day to read out the names of those who fell in both wars. As he did so, he could not help noticing Helen Sanderson, Ted's widow and the Commander's mother, weeping silently as she remembered the men who had fallen whom she had known when they were but children.

The names of the dead were read out every year on Armistice Day until the practice was ceased in 1976, after the final retirement from the school of Brian Hewitt, one of the school's legendary and long-serving masters. The reading of the names also had a profound effect on young Sebastian Faulks, who was later inspired to write *Birdsong* (1993):

> I had been thinking about the First World War off and on since the day when, as a schoolboy of twelve, I was asked to read out loud during assembly on 11 November the names of the old boys of my school who had died in the two world wars. It was a tiny school, but the list was so long that I was excused lessons the next day with a sore throat. Something had clearly gone on, I thought, something unspeakable. When the history teacher, so forthcoming on the Corn Laws and the Stuarts, came to the subject of the Great War, he seemed to struggle for breath.[89]

In 1917, the school won two top scholarships at Harrow and Westminster. Rationing was introduced in January that year, but despite that, the average weight of the boys increased by 3lb per head. The football team were unbeaten, and in one cricket match, Baucher Senior took ten wickets for one run, a feat recorded in *The Field*. Towards the end of the war, Joseph Conrad praised Ted Sanderson for his 'great achievement' in running Elstree. Soon after this, Ted, whose health was never strong, took a cure from April until July 1918.

Peacetime Again

Denis Ian Duveen (1910–1992), at the school from 1918 to 1923, was a chemist, entrepreneur, orchid grower and chemistry historian. He went on to Rugby and Merton College, Oxford, and in due course became a chemist at the Royal Gunpowder Factory at Waltham. Later, he emigrated to the US and founded the Duveen Soap Corporation on Long Island, finally settling in Brazil.

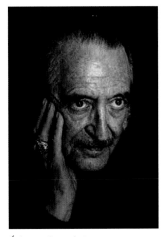

Édouard Roditi

In 1919, Édouard Roditi (1910–1992), an American poet, whose father was a Sephardic Jew, was sent to Elstree from a well-heated house in Paris. He found the place distinctly glacial in contrast, and suffered regularly from chilblains and a chronic cold. He assumed his father wanted to convert him into an English gentleman. He had never had much to do with British youth and experienced his 'first rough contacts with upper-class English boys' of his own age. He found their language violent, the whole experience 'shocking', concluding: 'Though [his school years] prepared me for life in the Twentieth-century world of increasingly brutal "interpersonal relations", they left me for many years with a profound distaste for almost everything, with the notable exception of orange marmalade, that comes from the British Isles.'[90] Nevertheless, he still preferred Elstree to Charterhouse and Balliol College, Oxford.[91]

One afternoon in the summer of 1920, Ted Sanderson spotted him in the yard and, as he needed to talk to some school parents, asked him to talk to 'Mr Conrad', who was visiting him. Roditi had never heard of Conrad and encountered an 'elderly bearded man', a 'gentle, tired man', a 'modest, kindly old gentleman' as he variously described him. Conrad complimented him on speaking several languages, asked him about his home, his family and his hobbies, and suggested in a roundabout way that he might perhaps follow in his footsteps and write in a language that was not his native tongue. This Roditi did, but, as he confessed, he was sadly too young to recall the other things this great literary figure told him. One of the masters told him how impressed he was to see him talking to Conrad.* It is not every prep school that could produce such figures.[92]

There were other distinguished old boys from Ted Sanderson's time as headmaster. Ronald Barton, CBE (at Elstree 1914–16) became the doyen of the British wine community in the Bordeaux region. Born in 1902, he went on to Eton and New College, Oxford. He moved to Château Langoa in 1924 and for most of his life was the head of Barton & Guestier, founded in 1725 by his ancestor, Thomas Barton. He spoke immaculate French and used his OE tie to hold up his white flannels on the real tennis court. He died in 1986.

Lord May of Weybridge sent his son Patrick to the school between 1919 and 1924. According to school records, though not mentioned in any of the biographies or the famous autobiography, *The Moon's a Balloon*, the actor David Niven was at the school between 1919 and 1921.† Rt Hon. Sir Roger Ormrod (at Elstree 1921–4) rose to be a Lord Justice of Appeal. He was born in 1911 and died in 1992. Lord Walston (at Elstree 1922–5) (formerly Waldstein) was a Liberal politician who later joined the Labour party and the SDP. A well-known agriculturalist, he is best remembered for the long affair his wife Catherine had with the writer Graham Greene, which was immortalised in Greene's 1951 novel *The End of the Affair*.

---

* Joseph Conrad died in Canterbury in August 1924.

† Niven wrote that he was at a hated school in Worthing, but was removed from there and sent to Heatherdown. In fact, he went from Elstree to Heatherdown. After being expelled, he evidently attended a school for difficult boys run by a Commander Bollard. Niven went to Stowe in September 1923, not long after it opened.

Domestic Staff, 1921

In September 1921, J.F. Walmsley came to the school from Clare College, Cambridge, having previously been at Dover College under Revd Lushington. He took the top form in English, taught classics during the Second World War, succeeded W.G. Byron as dormitory master, and in 1940 became a lay reader, responsible for the chapel services. His eyesight had prevented ball games at university, though he had rowed for his college. In 1949, his eyesight collapsed, and he had to resign. He went blind, spending twenty years in retirement in Bexhill and later in south Devon. He died on 16 January 1970.

In 1926, Ted Sanderson appointed Brian Hewitt as a schoolmaster, telling his son that he had made an excellent appointment. Hewitt came to the school for a year and stayed there for the rest of his working life. He had been born in Surbiton on 19 April 1904. His father had worked on the London Stock Exchange and had left him a fortune which helped. He hated the telephone, on which he was notably monosyllabic: 'Can't talk. Ring later.'

Brian Hewitt (known to some boys as 'Hubbo') took infinite care over every aspect of school life. He was remembered for his idiosyncratic expressions such as 'Well done, Sir' to those who made good efforts, 'On speed, now, Sir' to tardy boys, the use of words such as 'bide', 'yea' and 'nay', and enquiries about the health of a boy's 'Pater'. If he felt that some boy was particularly hopeless, he would declare: 'Why, the fellow's a lunatic', and suggest the possibility that he be sent to 'The Prewitt', a reference to Park Prewitt, the psychiatric hospital, just north of Basingstoke. At Woolhampton, he would greet the groundsman, John Veres, with a 'Heigh-ho, Johann'. While the school passage was pervaded with the smell of the matron's coffee,

Brian Hewitt

the tiny common room for teaching scholars was filled with the smoke of Hewitt's pipe.

Boys went to Hewitt for Latin, which would be their first lesson of the day. He was responsible for the sports programme for most of his forty-five years at the school, arranging some twenty-one sports days, and succeeding in making all the preliminary heats 'tremendous fun for all taking part'. He would start every race with his well-recognised shooting stick, used to encourage the boys on their way. During his time at Old Elstree in the 1930s, he trained tremendous football sides, which seldom lost a match. In 1927, the football team won all their matches for the second year running, which was attributed to Mr Hewitt's training. David Cooper described him as 'a wonderful character who aged early' and the 'Mr Chips' of Elstree.

He was well remembered by the boys. Andrew Birkin described him as 'a slightly eccentric, genial and amusing figure, who spoke in antiquated terms', while Tim Christie found him 'a lovely human being and a good teacher'. Robert Fellowes thought that, effectively, Hewitt ran the school, with Ian Sanderson as a kind of non-executive chairman. He certainly ran the school for two terms in 1957 when Sanderson was ill.

Hewitt was still teaching French in the 1970s. Charles Riley recalled: 'He instilled "Mon, Ma, Mes, Son, Sa, Ses" into us by declining these pronouns in a sing-song voice.'[93] He could also be severe. When a boy was in trouble, he would whack the hard end of his pipe on his head (or 'nut' as he called it) or make him stand in the wastepaper basket into which he hurled bits of chalk.

When Hubbo retired, Ian Sanderson wrote: 'Elstree will never seem the same without this splendid master, who has so quietly, modestly, humorously, wisely, and above all, so kindly helped some eight hundred little boys on their five year journey from their nurseries to their Public Schools.'[94] He gave his whole working life to Elstree.*

* * * * *

Illness was prevalent at the school in the 1920s and the 1930s. Whooping cough in the Easter term of 1923 meant that services were held in the Big Schoolroom on two occasions. There was more illness in the Easter term of 1924, meaning Holy Communion could only be celebrated on five Sundays. In 1928, an epidemic of measles postponed confirmation and brought the term to an end a fortnight early. The following year, school services were held in the Big Schoolroom due to an outbreak of influenza. Only half the school were fit. Then, in the summer of 1932, three or four cases of scarlet fever were diagnosed. On 1 June, R.D.G.E. Ware died of meningitis at the age of ten, his urn being placed in the north wall of the chapel. In the Lent term of 1938, only six boys were confirmed due to whooping cough.

In 1925, a dinner was given by Sir Frederick Wise MP and his wife at Holwell Court, Hatfield, and the decision taken to form an Old Elstree Club, advanced by Patrick Wise, who became chairman. The club's first dinner was held on 8 January 1926 at the Trocadero, with membership already at forty-eight alumni. In later years, this would morph into the Elstree School Association.

The school chapel continued to be a major feature of school life. At the end of the Michaelmas term of 1928, R.L. Otter-Barry (at Elstree

---

* (Charles) Brian (Griffiths) Hewitt died on 14 February 1989 in New Donnington Hayes Nursing Home. In 1984, when he was eighty, one of the school gardeners hailed him as 'an octogeranium'. Lord Bramall read one of the lessons at his memorial service.

1924–7) presented a porcelain plaque to the chapel, 'in memory of three happy years'. At Easter 1932, electric light was installed in the chapel, with twelve floodlights at the height of the eaves and a light in the sanctuary and the choir. These were the gift of R.S. Johnson (at Elstree 1926–31), who left for Harrow. The Very Revd Albert Baillie, Dean of Windsor, preached in the Lent term of 1933 and James Alexander (Sandy) Sanderson (born 31 January 1931), son of Commander Ian, was baptised there. On 4 June 1934, a service was held in the chapel for Ted's sister, Monica Lushington, whose ashes were deposited in a new recess in the south wall of the chancel. In 1937, a new altar frontal was presented by Revd Lushington and his daughter, Evelyn.

The Silver Jubilee of King George V in the summer of 1935 and his death in January 1936 were both recognised by the school. The future playwright Sandy Wilson was confirmed in the chapel in December 1936, and in the summer of 1938, the Revd E.E.A. Heriz-Smith was pleased to record more communicants in the school chapel than any previous term, with a total of 114. The Michaelmas term of 1936 was somewhat overshadowed by the political crisis, and it seemed to many that the outbreak of war was inevitable.

* * * * *

Amongst the old boys, the school produced several courtiers – Rear Admiral Sir Christopher Bonham Carter (at Elstree 1915–21), who was Prince Philip's private secretary from 1970 until his death in 1975. He was born in 1907. Sir Philip Hay (at Elstree 1926–31) was Princess Marina's private secretary from 1948 until her death in 1968. He was born in 1918 and died in 1986. He was a prisoner of war of the Japanese during the Second World War.

The 7th Marquess Townshend (1916–2010) succeeded to the title in 1921 when he was five years old. He was at the school in 1929. He had the unfortunate experience of coming of age on 13 May 1937, the day after George VI's coronation. His predicament was the subject of considerable correspondence, but the conclusion was that he was not allowed to take his place amongst the marquesses, though he was given a seat in Westminster Abbey.

The Early 1930s

The period between 1933 and 1938 is exceptionally well covered, thanks in part to the fact that three of the old boys from this time led prominent lives, two survived the Second World War, and one wrote his memoirs.

Sandy Wilson

Sandy Wilson (1924–2014) was the writer of several successful musicals, most famously the musical comedy *The Boy Friend* (1954). His direct contemporaries were Edwin (Dwin) Bramall, later Field Marshal Lord Bramall, KG, Chief of the Defence Staff (1924–2019), after whom the Bramall Sports Hall was named, and Squadron Leader Christopher Blount, MVO (born 1925), an equerry to Queen Elizabeth II in the 1950s, and a governor of the school for many years.

Sandy Wilson

Wilson was at the school between 1933 and 1937. His father, George Wilson, was the youngest son of a Scotsman who had made a fortune in the woollen mills industry and bought Bannockburn House. They lived well in India, but by the time they returned to England, the family fortunes were at low ebb. Sandy's birth in 1924 was regarded as a stress on the family's already strained resources.

Sandy's father had been to Harrow, where he had been captain of the football team. A place awaited Sandy in the headmaster's house, but given the lack of funds, he needed a substantial scholarship. Sandy's paternal aunt was a friend of Helen Sanderson. The aunt's husband contributed to the fees, and Sandy was admitted to Elstree on condition that he learned to box.

Before he set off, his sister advised him never to swank or to call any boy by his Christian name. His father told him that if anyone bullied him, he should announce: 'My father was Captain of Football at Harrow', which he claimed would silence them.

Sandy arrived at Elstree, travelling with his mother on the London Underground and then by bus. He found Helen Sanderson 'a gracious and handsome lady not unlike Ethel Barrymore, with a penchant for Pekingese'.[95] He was horrified at his first sight of a urinal and that the lavatory cubicles had no doors. After meeting Ted Sanderson, the headmaster, by then 'a distinguished white-haired gentleman with a military bearing',[96] he passed through the green baize door to the school side, where a noise like a cattle stampede indicated that the other pupils had arrived. One older pupil greeted him: 'Hello, new squit! What's your name?' He replied: 'Alexander Galbraith Wilson, and my father was Captain of Football at Harrow.'[97]

Sandy wrote: 'The five years I spent at Elstree were on the whole the most disagreeable of my life and looking back on them now I am amazed to think that I endured them with hardly a murmur of complaint, as indeed did most of the boys who were there with me.'[98] He found the food appalling and inadequate, with the last meal of the day at 6 p.m. consisting of bread and jam, and tea (though some parents paid extra for eggs). The general undernourishment meant that epidemics broke out. A specialist was called in, as a result of which a hot meal was prescribed for tea, and they were given Ovaltine and biscuits before bedtime. But lunches on Wednesdays and Saturdays were still boiled mutton (christened 'Polly' after the ancient school horse), with boiled greens, followed by tapioca or sago. The first half of the meal had to be eaten in silence.

Sandy considered that the savings on food were spent on employing excellent masters: 'The standard of teaching was exceptional and the school's claim of a high scholarship rate was certainly justified.'[99] But he did not care for the general routine of sport, football or rugby in the winter, cricket in the summer, and 'long and tedious walks in crocodile formation, not through the fields and woods in the neighbourhood, but along the featureless arterial roads which surrounded Elstree.'[100] Breaktime consisted of going out to a gravelled yard to kick a football about. On Saturdays, there was a lantern lecture and, towards the end of his school time, a film. The general boredom was alleviated by Miss Davies, who ran a club for the boys. The boys were allowed to chat or read for ten minutes before bedtime. Ablutions were carried out in total silence.

The dormitories were named after heroes of the Great War, such as Haig, French, Beatty and Jellicoe. Sandy's dormitory was called Horne for a reason he did not understand.* The sick bay was called Egypt, after the home of the Ten Plagues. The school day ended when Miss Tate, the school housekeeper, 'a formidable woman with hefty thighs and a sloping shelf of bosom',[101] appeared with jangling keys to tell them to: 'Settle down now, everybody and go to sleep.'

One of the joys of being a schoolmaster must be to spot the early talent of one of the pupils and to follow their subsequent career. Sandy Wilson's future life developed from the dreams and fantasies he conjured while lying in his Elstree dormitory. While at school, he dreamt of creating musicals, even composing a song called 'Love is Like a Pretty Maiden'. His talent was richly rewarded in his later life.

Field Marshal Lord Bramall & Christopher Blount

During the writing of this book, two old boys who lived on from the days of the first Elstree were Field Marshal Lord Bramall and Christopher Blount.

Christopher Blount recognised the early ambition to be found in his contemporary Dwin Bramall. He remembered him saying at school that it was his ambition to be chief of the British Army. In an immensely respected military career – the historian Sir Alistair Horne wrote that 'Dwin has had a charmed life'[102] – he was spotted by Field Marshal Lord Carver as a future Chief of the Defence Staff nine years before the post was his. He was the last Chief to have served in the Second World War, taking part in the Normandy landings, and being personally decorated with the Military Cross by Field Marshal Viscount Montgomery of Alamein. He held numerous positions of importance in Great Britain and was appointed a Knight of the Garter in 1990.

Lord Bramall's parents were not especially well-off, but sent him to day school at Gibbs in London. His grandparents then paid his Elstree fees. He arrived at the school in January 1935, when he was ten years old. His

---

* General Henry Sinclair Horne, 1st Baron Horne, GCB, KCMG (1861–1929) was a British artillery officer, considered the unknown general of the First World War. He served with Field Marshal Lord Haig and played a substantial part in the Battle of Somme.

biographer noted: 'Academically, he was no better than average, giving his greatest enthusiasm to sports and games.' He was one of many who described the school as being run by Commander Sanderson ('no intellectual') like a ship. School was severe in his day. He hated going back there and would be unable to sleep, hearing a church bell every quarter of an hour. The school train left St Pancras at 6.05 p.m. He recalled that there was no excuse if your parents' car broke down bringing you back to school after an occasional day out: 'You had to be back for the Sunday afternoon service. If your parents' car had a puncture,

Lord Bramall in the robes of the Order of the Garter

that was no excuse. You were liable to be beaten.' He echoed Sandy Wilson in appreciating the quality of the masters, maintaining that any economies they made over the school food were clearly invested in appointing good masters: 'The food was pretty rudimentary. Your parents could pay for an extra egg.' The yard was seared in his memory, particularly the loos with no doors. (The euphemism for a visit there was 'Playing in the yard'.) Robert Stainton, a classical scholar who taught there between 1934 and 1938, was a particular hero amongst the masters. He once caught him rushing downstairs: 'Bramall. Don't come rushing down. Go back up and come down properly.'[103]

Bramall captained the school cricket side and made two centuries not out in his second season.[104] He retained an unbeaten batting average of ninety-seven. He enjoyed boxing, which they practised at Wellington Barracks, with guardsmen acting as seconds. He also enjoyed rugby and football, recalling that as he came off the rugby field after a match, one of them, an Oxford double-blue and classical scholar, upbraided him: 'Bramall, you funked that tackle!' He remembered those words as he was about to land on the beach at Normandy and it gave him strength.[105]

After his time at Elstree, Dwin Bramall hoped to have gone on to Harrow, but his parents chose Eton instead.

July 1937, The Eleven. BACK ROW: N.G. Andrews, R.J. Pratt, P.C. Williams, J.B. Ewart, T.R.C. Walker FRONT ROW: C.C. Blount, The Earl of Mount Charles, E.N.W. Bramall, P.H.L. Scott, G.H. Johnson (not in the picture, A.E. Weatherall)

Christopher Blount was the son of Air Vice Marshal C.H.B. Blount, who was killed in an air accident in October 1940. In later life, Christopher became an RAF pilot and was appointed as equerry to the Queen aged twenty-nine after serving as adjutant to 615 (County of Surrey) Royal Auxiliary Air Force at Biggin Hill. One of his duties involved hiding a decanter of whisky late at

Christopher Blount

night at Windsor Castle, but the Queen's uncle, the Duke of Gloucester, 'sniffed about – he knew it was there somewhere' and he found it hidden behind a curtain.

He remembered that Bob Stainton, senior classics master and a football blue at Oxford, later lived on an island in Greece, from which he emerged once a year and never stopped talking. Sandy Wilson used to be spotted drawing pictures of girls' dresses (a talent later put to good use in his productions). Christopher Blount disliked the compulsory boxing and was not

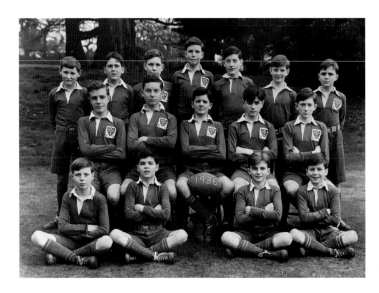

1936 rugby squad

displeased when he was hit on the nose by Lord Mount Charles, a fellow pupil, and disqualified. As for Commander Sanderson, he was 'not particularly academic … bleak but not unkind … beat hard enough … and never went out.'[106]

* * * * *

Sir Donald Hawley (1921–2008), a lawyer and diplomat who served in Dubai, Cairo, Lagos and Baghdad, and who ended his career as High Commissioner in Malaysia, was another Elstree old boy. He recalled that Ted Sanderson was known as 'Old Bags' and his son, Ian, as 'Young Bags'. The dormitory master, Mr Walmsley, meanwhile, was known as 'Warmers'. He remembered that the worst punishment was six strokes of the cane, something he avoided: 'I'm embarrassed to admit that I didn't receive it as it was considered rather wet not to be beaten.' He preferred school sausages to those at home. Steamed pudding was the regular dessert.

Another distinguished boy was Trevor Whitaker (1924–2018). He was born in Chelsea, the son of an officer in the Rifle Brigade and later the RAF. He was a contemporary of Field Marshal Bramall, both at Elstree and later at Eton. He then went to King's College, Cambridge, where his education was cut short by the war. In 1944, his unit landed in Normandy and made their way through the bocage country, near Caen, liberating the town of Flers. They advanced into the Netherlands, where Whitaker cleared road blocks under heavy mortar fire along the road south of Merselo, even after he had been wounded in the leg. Returning to his battalion after recuperation, he was one of the first soldiers to discover the horrors of the Belsen concentration camp after it was liberated. He described what he found: 'with the sick, dead and dying the compounds were not unlike a medieval portrayal of hell.' By the end of the Second World War, Whitaker had been awarded the Military Cross. In old age, he was made Chevalier of the Légion d'Honneur for having participated in the liberation of France.

One boy who did not come to the school was the son of Clement Attlee, the future British prime minister. In about 1937, Mrs Attlee asked Ian Sanderson to take her son as a day boy until her husband took office, but the Commander said: 'No – only boarders.'

* * * * *

There were eighty-four boys in 1933, but this number dwindled to forty by the time war broke out. At old Elstree, there used to be an annual cricket match between the masters and a team from the Coldstream Guards, and there was one football team that won every match in one particular term.

Ted Sanderson appointed Robert Stainton as assistant master in 1934. He remembered Ted as 'a strong yet skilled mentor, impressing on the newcomer, to whom he intended to entrust his beloved classics, the need for unremitting accuracy in grammar and syntax, and fluency in prose composition.' Ted valued honesty, responsibility, good manners and games. Stainton used to observe 'his thin ascetic face' taking delight when the school won a great victory on the playing field.[107]

At that time, the classics were all important, Latin and Greek being essential for admission to the great public schools. In 1931, two inspectors came and were impressed by the headmaster's enthusiasm for the subject.

Music was overseen by David Beardwell (Beardie) (1869–1912), and following him a lady from Miss Verne's School of Music. From that school emerged Dorothy Davies, almost a concert pianist, who arrived in 1912 and taught the boys with vigour until her death in 1963. Helen Sanderson started a pack of Wolf Clubs in 1926, and Felix Greenwood, an old boy living in the village, instigated the Boy Scouts in 1928.

Between 1931 and 1938, all schools suffered from the financial burdens of the economic depression, and though Elstree survived while other schools floundered, there was no waiting list during those years.

Ted Sanderson had never enjoyed good health. He tended to catch the flu each winter, and he relied heavily on his wife, Helen, for support. In 1926, he obtained the lease of a house on Islay with its own shoot on the Mull of Oa. Here he fished in the loch, tackled salmon in the river and enjoyed the use of the first-class golf course nearby. This was where he spent his summer holidays. He retired from the school in 1935, amidst much feting. It was typical of his dedication to the last that even as the removal men emptied his study, he sat in the one remaining chair, correcting some Latin set book exam papers. His philosophy had always been to work right until the end of term.

Ted left the school in good condition. He and Helen moved to Saunton in Devon, where he enjoyed four years of retirement. As his health was poor, Helen wanted him to be out of England for the winter. Sadly, a visit to Kenya in 1938 proved too much for him. He stayed in Devon for another year, but died of influenza on 23 March 1939, just before the school moved to Woolhampton.

Ted was judged to have been an outstanding headmaster. As *The Times* put it after his death: 'Sanderson was a man of many parts. A fine scholar, a keen and graceful athlete and sportsman, distinguished in presence and with many faithful friends, he will be chiefly remembered for his simple loyalty, his generosity, and the complete uprightness of his life.'[108] A memorial service was held for the 'Old Chief' on 28 March 1939. The chapel was filled with relations and beautifully decorated with flowers, with the service conducted by the chaplain, Revd Lushington and Revd Ridgeway.

His widow, Helen, lived on in nearby Bucklebury, sharing a home with her sister Peggy. The boys used to visit her well into the 1950s and found the two ladies keen to talk about religion. She died in 1967, at the age of ninety-two.

CHAPTER TEN

COMMANDER IAN SANDERSON, RN
(1900–1979)

HEADMASTER 1939–69

Ian Campbell MacDougall Sanderson (1900–1979) was the third generation of the family to take on the running of the school. He had been destined for the Royal Navy from an early age, and had served as a midshipman in the First World War.

He received early praise from Conrad, who wrote that he appreciated 'the sterling worth of Ian. He's the most sympathetic little man I've ever met in my life. I felt in touch with him as if he were my own.'[109]

Commander Ian C.M. Sanderson, RN

He was invariably known as 'the Commander', having served in the Royal Navy, which as Conrad put it, had brought him 'into line'. He was born in Newton Stewart, Wigtownshire, on 5 May 1900, educated at the Royal Naval Colleges of Osborne and Dartmouth, and was Cadet Captain and a member of the cricket XI at both schools. He went to sea aboard HMS *Malaya* in 1917 as a midshipman, and witnessed the surrender of the German High Seas Fleet at Scapa the following year. He arrived at King's College, Cambridge in 1921, as a naval officer, for a short course. He won the Squash Racquets Championship of the Royal Navy three times in the 1920s and was a playing member of the MCC. He retired from the Royal Navy in 1931 to help his father with the school.

Ian was to have two wives. The first was Louisa Constance Mackintosh, known as 'Moulie', whom he married at St George's, Hanover Square, in 1928. They had two sons and two daughters. The elder boy, John, lived in Ayrshire as a seaweed farmer with Alginate Industries after a life racing cars and farming in Africa. His younger brother, Sandy, followed his father into the Fleet Air Arm after Dartmouth. He was successful but was killed in a flying accident.

Robert Stainton found Ian's style different to that of his father, though they shared the same ideals: 'He brought with him a certain naval smartness and a punctilio that at first irritated

Louisa Constance
Mackintosh 'Moulie'

us, but he had a mellowing enthusiasm equal to his father's, although less intellectual.'[110] The Commander chose good staff, having learned of the necessity to do so in the navy; he was also a little freer in his approach to school life than his father, but made sure that discipline was paramount when it mattered. Though he himself knew no Greek, he placed a clock in the classics room with a Greek quotation: 'Six hours are quite enough for chores'. He was not officious and was always accessible. Even so, in those days, all masters were addressed by their surnames.

In the remaining years at old Elstree, weekends away from school were rare, as were visits from parents. During school weekends, boys were expected to organise their own amusements. Sunday afternoon walks were a less popular feature of weekends. Robert Stainton summed up the life there:

> In the thirties Elstree School was a place to serve and to enjoy, conservative perhaps – for we did not listen much to the rumbling premonitions of Europe – but strongly involved in the training of boys in mind, body, and spirit for whatever they might encounter in the outside world.
>
> I don't recall any inkling of the 'rat-race'; only of a 'slump' facing youth when it grew up, but this seemed at the time less real than our preoccupation

with the present. When London's expansion and the Second World War drove the school to Woolhampton, it would under Ian Sanderson, continue to show that a proper education is both timeless and adaptable to change, so long as it remains open and independent, and headmaster and staff are at one with parent and boy.[111]

Another old boy, Sir Richard Hanbury-Tenison, wrote that the Commander was 'still very much the naval officer and a bit remote from the boys'. He continued:

> The junior masters seemed to hold him in some awe. At least on one occasion that I recall he was less than clever. At the end of one term he called together the smaller boys, of which I was then one, to tell us that next term a new boy called Wragg, son of the then famous jockey,* would be coming to the school and that we were to be particularly kind to him. In fact I cannot imagine that any of us would have wanted to bully the son of a well-known jockey – we would be much likelier to have been impressed. In fact poor little Wragg *did* get off to a bad start, not because of his father but because his mother had sent him to school with combinations, rather than the normal vest and pants!
>
> I remember my father telling me long after that when he had called on Commander Sanderson before sending me up, he had asked what standard of work would be expected. To which the Headmaster replied: 'The only thing we insist on is that the boy should be able to write home to his mother!'
>
> I don't think we were under very much pressure and I managed to get through all of Henty and Stanley Weyman together with most of Rider Haggard. I have never been much good at games and I have a feeling that the general standard of games before the war was pretty low at Elstree. Chapel services were well done, I think, and I remember enjoying Evensong on summer evenings.[112]

Hanbury-Tenison remembered that the headmaster used to read out speeches from Stanley Baldwin, then prime minister, on the need to re-arm.

---

* Harry Wragg (1902–1985) became Champion Jockey in 1941, was the winner of thirteen British classics, and later became a successful trainer.

He marked this as 'the beginning of an interest in the outside world'.[113] At the end of the summer term, the chaplain, Revd Eustace E.E.A. Heriz-Smith, left to take up the vicarage of Radley.

War was imminent. Commander Sanderson and his wife began to explore some twenty possible sites to which to move the school, all within fifty miles of London, and they had their eye on Woolhampton, near Reading, as first choice. They entered into negotiations with its then owner, Countess Gurowska, whose husband, the Count, had died on 10 March that year. In April, the Countess put the house on the market, and Commander Sanderson secured a twenty-one-year lease.

It was just as well they did, because within two days of the outbreak of war on 3 September 1939, the British Army took possession of the school buildings at Old Elstree. The billeting officers arrived, and some 180 officers and men of the 11th HAC Regiment moved into Hill House the following day. It became imperative to move, and fortunately, Countess Gurowska was co-operative. She said that the school could come to Woolhampton as soon as her furniture was moved out.

Everything was moved except the school chapel and the squash courts. Barker's vans arrived on 14 September but were requisitioned. All the school paraphernalia had gone by 22 September.

Staff with Ian Sanderson and Brian Hewitt

PART TWO

CHAPTER ELEVEN

WOOLHAMPTON

The first indication that the school was moving came to parents and boys during the summer holidays of 1939. A letter arrived telling them that the school was moving from Elstree to Woolhampton.

One of the boys who made the move was Bill Tyrwhitt-Drake (1926–2008). After spending four years at the old Elstree, he had quite expected to return there in September 1939:

> We arrived in Woolhampton and somehow they had arranged for the transfer of a lot of the furniture and some of the equipment from Hertfordshire. In those days there was just the main house and the stable block although we didn't use the stable block. Three or four temporary classrooms were built at the back of the school and we used to play football there. I happened to be the Captain of Cricket (in 1940) and we had to play all our matches away because there wasn't a cricket pitch at all. They started a wicket where the present 1st XI pitch is now and we had one match at the very end of the season against the paters. This was, I believe, the first game of cricket to be played at Elstree.[1]

He explained the difference between the two schools:

> The school in Hertfordshire had its own swimming pool, squash courts and a large yard which we played on in breaks. It had a rifle range and a beautiful cricket ground with pavilion and a delightful chapel and then we came here. The conditions were Spartan. They just mowed a field for a cricket pitch and laid a rough square. We used to bathe in the larger of the two lakes, occasionally! The cricket nets were in the same position as they are today and there might have been a grass tennis court from when it was a country house. The lack of facilities was the main difference between the two schools.[2]

Nor was Tyrwhitt-Drake impressed by the food, but he recognised that he was at school in wartime.

The school's move was handled by Ian Sanderson with customary efficiency. They settled in easily, with the beginning of term delayed by only eight days. They found themselves in a safer part of the country and were happy to remain there, the school gradually developing and, in due course, expanding. However, it was primitive. A bathroom and lavatories had to be installed. The conservatory roof leaked and had to be replaced. Jim Champion had arrived at the old Elstree in 1933. Without a proper kitchen, he did all the odd jobs, even heating the water in a vast cauldron in the old boot room. At the new site, the grounds would not be fit for games until September 1940.

Woolhampton was originally Wulflafing-Tun to the Saxons, and named as Ollivintone by the Normans in the Domesday Book. It sits on the banks of the River Kennet, in a valley which stretches fifty miles from the Marlborough Downs to the Thames at Reading, and has been used as a thoroughfare for thousands of years.

Woolhampton House, East Front and Entrance, 1907

Woolhampton House, South Front, 1907

This was a route used for access to the west of England. In due course, it developed into the Great Bath Road, the Kennet and Avon Canal, and the Great Western Railway. (When the rail line extended from Reading to Hungerford in 1847, there was a station at Woolhampton; its name was changed to Midgham as rail users confused it with Wolverhampton.) A Roman road crosses nearby from Silchester to Cirencester.

As an increasing number of people used roads, rivers and rails as trading routes, many coaching inns were built along the way. Woolhampton itself was a well-known stopping place on the Great Bath Road (now the A4) on journeys from London to Bath, and was well-known for its coaching inns. The eighteenth-century Rowbarge Inn was originally built as a beer shop for the navvies who dug the canal and built Woolhampton Lock between 1718 and 1723. Still to this day, old painted signs survive on some of the buildings.

Inevitably, highwaymen lurked in wait for unsuspecting travellers, many of whom made their journeys with their valuables about them. Perhaps the most notorious was Captain 'Flying' Hawkes, an infamous character who employed a variety of disguises to deceive innocent travellers. One day, he disguised himself as a pious Quaker and intercepted a rich young blade at an inn at Slough. So taken in was the rich man that he boasted of his wealth and the power of his pistols. On the road to East Berkshire, Hawkes disarmed him and robbed him of his worldly goods. Hawkes settled at the Old Sun Inn (which later became the Rising Sun) at Woolhampton, delighted with his haul. Later, however, there was a brawl in the pub and he unwisely joined in. He found he had been tricked. Red-breasted Bow Street Runners were lying in wait for him, and he was arrested.

Up the hill, comfortably away from such adventures, stood Woolhampton House. The original manor of Woolhampton was bought by William Wollascot after the dissolution of the monasteries, and it remained in the Wollascot family until 1759. Over the years, they built much of the present building. There are even some remnants of the earlier Tudor building – some Tudor bricks near the garden door on the western front and several more in the old carpenter's shop, formerly the old laundry. There are also some rough frescoes in the attic rooms on the southern front, said to have been painted by a Roman Catholic chaplain to the Wollascot family whilst he was in hiding at a time of Catholic persecution.

William Wollascot, the last of the family, died without a male heir. His daughter and sole heiress, Henrietta, married the 7th Earl of Fingall, an Irish peer, in 1755. A few years later, in 1786, the Earl sold the estate to Mr John Crewe, of Bolesworth Castle, Cheshire.

Woolhampton House was to pass through several other owners. Crewe's daughter, Elizabeth (1764–1793), married the 3rd Viscount Falmouth, son of Admiral Rt Hon. Edward Boscawen (1711–1761), a famous naval figure, known as 'Old Dreadnought' and 'Wry-necked Dick'. Boscawen's wife was the celebrated Fanny Boscawen, whose letters have been published. She was a frequent visitor to Woolhampton. In 1856, the 6th Viscount sold Woolhampton House and 2,000 acres to James Blyth, a London merchant who lived in Park Lane and who had bought extensively in the area.

Blyth commissioned many alterations from an architect called John Johnson, who built a music room above the dining room, as well as adding the large conservatory and the pillared entrance porch and doors. In the nineteenth century, neighbouring Home Farm was built. Blyth died in 1873, but his daughters lived on there until 1907. It was then put on the market as 'the Woolhampton Estate', described as 'a comfortable and well-appointed Mansion, built of red brick with stone dressings'. It offered seventeen guest bedrooms with dressing rooms, bathrooms and servants' rooms, 'standing in a beautifully-timbered and boldly-undulating park, and surrounded by tastefully-arranged pleasure grounds'. There was a rookery, a lake and sixteen cottages, all in some 266 acres.[3]

In 1908, the house and 190 acres were sold to Major Dudley Melchior Beaumont, 4th Count Gurowski (1865–1939), son of the Austrian Consul in Nice. He married Hyacinthe von Essen (1878–1963), the half-Swedish granddaughter of the 8th Earl of Cavan. Two photographs of her by the fashionable photographer Bassano can be found in the archives of the National Portrait Gallery in London. The Gurowskis had three sons and a daughter, one son dying as a baby and two being killed in the Second World War within six months of each other, the first at Dunkirk.

Countess Gurowska

Aerial view

Gurowski (a count until 1920, when he renounced the title) was responsible for many of the finer features of Woolhampton House. He replaced the stone floor in the hall with oak, and introduced a fine oak staircase and panelling. He lengthened the southern front at both ends and redesigned the windows. He replaced the conservatory with a less ostentatious building, and ornamented the three main sides of the house with a white over-sailing cornice to relieve the severity of the red brick walls. He redirected the drive from its direct access to the Bath Road, to Cod's Hill, where he built another lodge and erected a magnificent archway, which is still there, but no longer the entrance to the estate.

When Gurowski died in March 1939, his widow put Woolhampton House on the market. Ian Sanderson could not afford to buy it, but attempted to lease it instead. At first, Countess Gurowska refused, but she eventually changed her mind. A twenty-one-year lease, with an option to buy at a later date for £15,000, was granted just in time for the move. The

Elstree East Front, 1939

95

Elstree South Front, 1939

Estate Working Party, 1940

lease was still being negotiated, and even before it was signed, the school moved in on 29 September. It was said that the Countess was moving out as the school moved in.*

---

* Countess Gurowska moved to Wargrave and died on 7 January 1963. When she died, Ian Sanderson wrote: 'She was a woman of rare beauty and distinction, and one likes to think this lovely place will always reflect some of the grace of the Countess whose home it was for 30 years.' She left £250 to the vicar and church wardens of Woolhampton to tend the family graves.

Front garden, 1955

Current South Front in the snow

Current panorama

Stable block

Church of St Peter's Woolhampton

Next to the school is the Church of St Peter, rebuilt in 1857, and a little further up the hill is Douai Abbey. When the Earl of Fingall moved to Ireland in 1786, he left his chaplain behind to minister to local Catholics. He was given seven acres of land. In 1829, a school was established and a chapel built, later replaced by St Mary's in 1848. In 1903, the Benedictine Community of St Edmund were expelled from Douai in France and were offered the site by the then Bishop of Portsmouth. They established the new Douai School there. The Abbey Church was built between 1928 and

Douai Abbey

1933 and completed as late as 1993. Douai School subsequently closed down.

Henry Brierly (1930–2001), later a vicar, was another boy who made the transition from Elstree to Woolhampton. He and his sister lived with the Sandersons when he was a boy, after his father died, since Ian Sanderson was his uncle. Evidently, they called him 'The Cheese' because there was always a large cheese on the headmaster's table and, seemingly, he was the only one allowed to cut pieces off it.

Harry Wragg, the famous jockey and trainer, sent his son, Geoff Wragg (1930–2017), to the school in about 1937. Geoff went on to Fettes, wanted to be a vet, but was fired by a lifelong interest in electronics when at Southampton University, working for a time as a radar engineer. He took over his father's licence at Abington Place, Newmarket in 1982, and trained for many owner-breeders. He produced many good winners, became one of the most respected trainers in horse racing, and enjoyed a sensational victory in the 1983 Derby with Teenoso, Lester Piggott's ninth and final victory in that race. He retired in 2008.

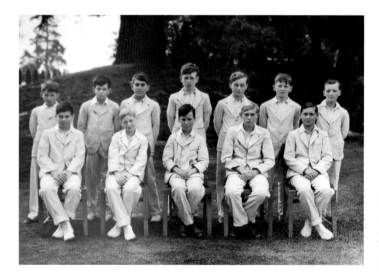

Henry Brierly (front row second left) and Geoff Wragg (front row right)

CHAPTER TWELVE

THE 1940s

Commander Sanderson had many problems to face. It had been thought that this school might not survive the economic crises of the 1930s, but it did. Following this, he had to cope with the war, which again threatened the long-term survival of the school. Hardly had they arrived at Woolhampton than there were air-raid practices in the cellar. A boy saw an air balloon shot down, and one evening there was an ominous bright orange glow in the direction of London. Later, Sanderson would have to face the exigencies of a Labour government. Despite this, Elstree weathered these various crises.

Harking back to his naval days, the Commander was inclined to ask his masters: 'Why aren't you ashore?' or 'What are you doing aboard?' At mealtimes, he walked around the dining room, straightening the backs of boys who were slouching. He was courageous, and in his life withstood a number of devastating personal misfortunes, coping with them aided by

Old Dining Room
(now the Staff
Common Room)

his strong Christian faith. He was a gifted man, both intellectually and athletically, and considered a fine schoolmaster. He inspired loyalty and respect, and had 'a delightful wit which had his friends in stitches in no time at all.'[4] Conversely, he could intimidate. Sebastian Faulks, at the school in the 1960s, described him as 'a tall, craggy, grey-haired man of terrifying demeanour'.[5]

Much is made these days of therapy and attention to minute detail, but the Commander was nothing if not astute when dealing with the boys and their parents. He kept notes on each pupil from the day the file was opened. He would meet the parents, and usually the boy too, when the child was perhaps five years old, despite the fact he would not be arriving at the school until he was eight. Nonetheless, the notes served to remind the Commander of his first impressions and any issues that were mentioned.

Sanderson was a more perspicacious judge of character than his naval life might imply. Some boys entered the school well balanced, with good reports behind them and full of enthusiasm, but others inspired more lively descriptions. Of two brothers, he wrote: 'When the two boys came, they were uncivilised, just like two puppies, but they are now fairly well behaved.' He noted: 'They are looked after at Upper Norwood by a charming scatter-brained old great aunt.'[6]

Other reports make entertaining though sometimes alarming reading: 'He is too fond of his food' and he 'lacks the true scholar's fire'; he is 'very dreamy and laid-back'; 'a nervous child, terrified of boarding school. Wets his bed once a week'; 'said to be livelier than his brother'; 'there are brains on his mother's side and great ability on his father's'; 'said to be like a newly opened champagne bottle'; 'believed to have been very unsettled after divorce of parents, which shows itself in arguing, sullenness and lying'; 'did not at all want to leave home and come to Elstree'; and 'bursts into tears far too easily, will never admit himself to be in the wrong and is terrified of games, which he loathes. Obviously this boy will need careful management'. One boy had been 'in trouble for putting objects down W.C. drains both at home and at school incurring large plumbers' bills.'[7]

Old boys from this era had their particular memories. The parents of George Eve (at Elstree 1945–50) were told by Sanderson that George had

102

no hope of passing the Common Entrance exam. Yet he passed into his next school in the top stream. He recalled hot and dusty walks to the grand and freezing Douai pool, where no swimming trunks were worn. Julian Fane (at Elstree until 1952) was sent to Elstree because his father and Sanderson had been midshipmen together in the First World War. He was beaten once, and noted that the worst part was being sent to the headmaster's study by one of the other masters, who then waited outside to listen.

Sanderson did not only have to deal with the boys; there were also the masters. A little later on, in 1947, the Archbishop of Canterbury wrote to him asking him his opinion of a man who had taught briefly at the school and subsequently applied to be a deacon or even a priest. Sanderson was unimpressed. The man in question had arrived for a term and immediately given notice, with talk of going to Buenos Aires. The headmaster gave a subtly dismissive verdict: 'In some positions he might serve the church but I cannot say I know of one and I would say he was too much of an oddity to become a good parish priest. In saying this, Your Grace, I am aware that I may be a very poor judge. I was brought up a sailor.'[8]

Fewer Elstree old boys died in the Second World War than in the Great War. Ian Sanderson recorded details of those who died or went missing. He listed thirty-four killed, many in the Middle East, many flying, as well as some in Sicily, Libya, Italy and North West Europe. Amongst these, Robin Farmiloe died of wounds in Syria serving with the London Rifle Brigade. There was no news of Captain Eric Dance (1900–1943), of the Royal Artillery, after Singapore fell. He was the son of Sir George Dance, a prolific and successful songwriter, and the older brother of James Dance, later an MP, who was also at Elstree. Eric became an actor and co-director of the Oxford Playhouse, without whose vision it would never have existed. He died in New Guinea on 30 April 1943, as a prisoner of war of the Japanese.

Lieutenant E.E.A. Chetwynd-Talbot (1920–1941), who had been awarded the George Cross for dealing with an unexploded bomb, and then appointed an MBE for disposing of a further bomb in Malta, went missing whilst out there on special duty with the RAF. He was finally presumed to have died in October 1941. His commanding officer commended him for his qualities of leadership and unassuming manner: 'And I happen to know that his bravery was not of the unimaginable, animal variety. He could be just as frightened as the rest of us, but it didn't show.'[9]

Alfred Fane had risen to the top ranks of motor racing drivers and was an amateur bull-fighter. He was lost on RAF operations in July 1942. He was described in tributes as having 'a most intelligent and thoughtful mind', having been 'a delightful and gifted friend', and destined 'to make his name known in a wider sphere'.[10] Lieutenant David Milling RE was killed in a motor accident in India, to which he had embarked with his commando unit in November 1942. His commanding officer cited his 'uprightness of character and quiet unassuming competence'.[11]

Several were taken prisoner, among them Philip Hay, who worked on the railroads in Burma for three and a half years. Some were noted as wounded or missing. More positively, the Commander noted several awards of Distinguished Service Crosses and Military Crosses.

One event not recorded in Ian Sanderson's album of happenings at the school was the personal tragedy he suffered in the summer of 1941. The body of his dark and glamorous wife Louisa (known as 'Moulie'), then living at 4 Hyde Park Place, W2, was identified on 15 May. She had died in the famous bomb attack on the Café de Paris on 8 May.* She was with her lover at the time when a fifty-kilogram high-explosive bomb hit the building.† This affected the Commander badly; when he announced her death, unsurprisingly, he requested: 'No letters, please.'[12]

In 1944 Agnes Mabel Hart, always known as Anne, came to teach at Elstree and continued to do so until the following year. Commander Sanderson married her in 1947. Anne Sanderson was a great organiser and an avid letter writer.

Anne Sanderson

---

* In his book, Ian Sanderson wrote that Louisa died when a bomb destroyed the house in which she was staying the night in London.

† At least thirty-four people died and dozens more were seriously injured in this incident. The basement and ground floor areas were only half-full at the time, as the bomb fell at about 9.45 p.m. Had it struck an hour later, many more people would have died.

She was zealous in keeping in touch with parents when a boy was ill, and she kept an eye on homesick boys or those who took a while to settle into school life.

She read to the lower school in her drawing room on Sunday evenings, the boys sitting cross-legged on her floor whilst the Commander read to the senior boys in his study. She wrote and produced school plays for both the senior and junior schools. Later, she taught scripture and explained the Bible stories. She particularly enjoyed the garden, and was saddened when, later, the rose garden was reduced in size. Nor did her herbaceous border survive by the old entrance to the school.* David Cooper recalled that parents were more scared of Anne Sanderson than they were of the headmaster.

Ben Hay was a perceptive observer of the school, with his combined role as a pupil and also being a Sanderson descendant. He arrived there in September 1949, staying until March 1955, and has captured the essence of what kept Elstree consistently high in the league of prep schools:

> The two qualities of the Sandersons (and their wives) were an unswerving determination to be the best and the ability to choose and retain good teachers, in the classroom and on the playing field. Loyalty was a virtue rewarded. Standards were set high. These qualities were founded on a strong Christian faith, not only of their own but of their wives. None of this was rammed down our throats but Prayers and the weekend Services in Woolhampton Church were a natural part of our lives. This endured through the three generations of the family and enabled them to weather the storm which followed Johnny Royle's departure and Lancelot's failing health.[13]

The Sandersons liked to consider that the school was run with a familial atmosphere, but this was tinged with the fear of the cane. Ben Hay outlined what he thought were the school's crucial qualities, begun with the Sandersons and carried through to the present day:

> Sound teaching, at scholarship level if necessary and sport of high standard; a Christian upbringing based on The Ten Commandments, which we learnt

---

* Anne stayed on in Lavenham after Ian died. However, arthritis made her final years difficult. When her eyesight also failed, she went into a nursing home. She died in 1994, aged eighty-nine.

by heart. Art and dancing (i.e. learning to waltz, the quick step and so on were then part of a young gentleman's education) were peripheral but they were there. Music was encouraged. And there was singing practice for choir and congregation. When one entered Miss Davies's room for a piano lesson, she made one sing middle D and marked each attempt on a sketched archery target – each ring for a flat or sharp off note! Enlightened too was a policy of allowing a music lesson to take the place of a subject lesson, thus not forcing musicians to give up games. The Sandersons were good at both and that helped.[14]

Miss Dorothy Davies

The fact that the school had but seventy boys, all boarding for twelve or thirteen weeks, gave the school something of a family feeling. Ben Hay continued:

The grounds were there for playing about, with fishing in the two ponds, and skating on them if it froze. In the Boy Scouts we learnt about the weather, woodcutting, camping with biscuit tin ovens and so on. I was lucky to be recruited as Mole Catcher's Assistant. That duty absolved one from the

Early ice skating days on the big lake

106

boring morning crocodile exercise walk. Fine leg on the cricket field had to pick his way between tens of mole hills if we failed in our trapping. But we became quite expert and aspired to a moleskin waist coat from the many bodies we skinned in the garage. A smelly corner and nowhere near enough for a coat.

From time to time we were paraded in our boiler suits to sweep up autumnal leaves and make bonfires or to pick fruit in the summer, gooseberries being the least favourite – too sour to eat and prickly. By today's standards the food was pretty rough – basically mutton in various forms all week with fish on Friday. If one failed to finish everything on one's plate, one was sent to the lift shaft outside Miss Davies's room to finish it off. You can squash quite a lot of mutton fat into a handkerchief but banana custard, which I couldn't eat, runs everywhere! Eventually a kind waitress took pity. One forgets, however, that the war in Europe had only ended three years before I went to Elstree and so there was still rationing. We were rarely ill and lived an energetic life; we were probably very lucky in what we had.

Ian had a shooting brake with a hole in the floor through which the exhaust sometimes escaped. In it we travelled to football and cricket matches, one boy being responsible for keeping his foot over the hole. He didn't always remember. The brake was driven by Bruno, Ian's chauffeur and loader. David Cooper used eventually to draw the line at us singing 'Bruno's driving dangerously, We'll soon be in the ditch' to the tune of 'All Go Marching On'. Chocolate biscuits were given to everyone at tea if we won.

Whilst a lively lot we knew that a toenail over the line would land us in the head's study for a whacking with 'butter pat', a flat instrument made by Carpie or, in case of serious transgression, with the cane. At the end of my first year, in July 1950, the head boy, a strapping lad called 'Borrett' stood as usual to say Grace before the whole school in the dining room:

'For what we are about to receive, may … Old Ma Kent be thoroughly ashamed of herself'.

This breach of etiquette and its ensuing favourable reception by all but the top table of masters earned Borrett a tap on the shoulder after lunch and six of the best just two hours before his parents were due to take him away for ever. Discipline was discipline. Nothing sentimental interfered. And the

Head Boy, Borrett
(front row, second
from the left)

combination of being rude about the cook and tampering with a prayer was certain suicide.[15]

Peter Vereker* arrived at Elstree in 1949, sent there because his father had been in the Royal Navy with Commander Sanderson. He was later to pursue a most individual, successful and varied career, but found himself 'dreadfully homesick', and so he ran away on the first day of his third term. He ran down to Midgham station and crouched down below the level of the train's carriage window because he had spotted the school doctor on the opposite platform:

> When I arrived home my mother drove me straight back, and Sanderson, whom I had expected to beat me, said that I was the only boy who had ever run away from Elstree and enquired whether I disliked the school food. He later made me the Head Boy, but I always found him an intimidating figure.[16]

In fact, he left the school 'laden with prizes for both work and games'.[17] In due course, twenty Verekers went to Elstree. When Peter Vereker brought

---

* Peter Vereker (1939–2001) became Ambassador and UK Permanent Representative to the Organisation for Economic Co-operation and Development (OECD) in Paris from 1995 to 1999. His *Telegraph* obituary described him thus: 'The thrusting, ambitious young Turk of the 1960s matured into a philosophical, friendly family man of great good humour, glad – so he wrote in the 1990s – to have escaped the syndrome which afflicted some of his colleagues: *la carrière réussie, la vie privee manquée*.' He died from a sudden heart attack, about to take part in a 36-hole golf tournament.

Peter Vereker
(back row right)

his son Connel there in 1979, he was pleased to find that there was 'a new, gentler, more sensitive regime in place, in accordance with the changing times'.[18]

Over the years, it was a tribute to the school how many fathers (and one mother) who had been at the school later sent their sons there. For example, there were several generations of Partridges, including John Partridge, the Bond Street antique dealer.

CHAPTER THIRTEEN

THE 1950s

The arrival of David Cooper in 1950 was a significant moment in the school's history. He came to the school thanks to Revd R.J.B. Eddison and their mutual involvement with Christian camps at Swanage. In July 1950, Eddison was going to approach a number of schools on Cooper's behalf. He started with Elstree as first choice, and Ian Sanderson replied: 'I would be interested in your young man if he's v.g. at games.'[19] Eddison wrote to Cooper, then serving as a 2nd Lieutenant at Carnoustie in Scotland: 'You could hardly do better. It's a tip-top school with a very good reputation … There is no need at this stage to go into details or what you can teach.'[20]

David Cooper

Sanderson invited David Cooper over, and by 26 July, he had confirmed his offer of a job at £200 a year, starting in September. Once he had accepted the job, the headmaster addressed him (informally) as 'Dear Cooper'. He was to teach maths to Form 7, geography to Forms 2, 3 and 6, English to Form 5, as well as scripture and catechisms. He was also to take on football, formerly in the care of Brian Hewitt from 1925 to 1947.

Cooper's parents lived in Ealing, where he was born on 12 July 1930. He was educated at Bradfield, where he played in the cricket and football First XIs, captaining the latter in 1948.

Revd R.J.B. Eddison

He completed his national service in the Royal Artillery. He never took a driving test, but finding himself stationed at Redford Barracks outside Edinburgh, he obeyed his battery commander's request to drive him into the city, after which he was given a document permitting him to drive. He went on to St John's College, Cambridge, where he read geography and played for the Falcons and for the Old Bradfieldians (in the Arthur Dunn Cup).

At first, he was referred to as 'the boy' (as junior masters were then called) and was lodged in a small room that had been the headmaster's dressing room. His last meal of the day was high tea with the boys. He was given no supper, so he fortified himself with cornflakes before he went to bed. After graduating from Cambridge, he returned to the school in 1954, and from then it became his life.

David Cooper himself recalled that he ran football and cricket, and taught the upper school Latin and the lower school mathematics. He was dormitory master, living in a little bedsit room that was located in the sick bay, very much on call. Everything was primitive when he was first there. The upper dormitory had no central heating, there were washstands with a bowl that would be filled by the school maids, and the school itself was heated by twenty-six coal fires. Every boy had a chamber pot.

Breakfast was at 7.30 a.m., served in the old conservatory, which Cooper recalled as 'baking hot in summer, freezing in winter'. There were ancient

David Cooper in his classroom

classrooms, with twelve boys in each, and main assembly was in the library. Cooper described Ian Sanderson as 'a very good headmaster of the old kind. He ran Elstree like a ship and never changed anything.'[21] Cooper's salary rose from £1,414 a year to £2,442 plus £100 as deputy headmaster in 1974; by 1995, he was being paid £32,001 a year.

Known as 'Kips' or 'DC', he kept friends all over the world. During the school holidays, he always had his golf clubs in the boot of his car. He toured the country, staying with old boys and playing golf whenever the chance arose.

He completed 129 terms at the school, a feat only superseded by Brian Hewitt. He served as assistant headmaster, head of geography and scripture, and master in charge of football (for thirty-nine years), hockey and cricket. He made and designed the golf course, opened up the cellar as Cellar Clubs, and started the skiing parties. He was also film projectionist on Saturday evenings. He masterminded a popular stool-weaving course for the boys, in which they assembled the stool, varnished it and wove it. Once completed, he would roll up his trousers and sit on the stool to test its construction.

A committed Christian since boyhood, he attended the Christian camps founded by Revd. R.J.B. Eddison – run first at Swanage and later at Monkton Combe – every year for over fifty consecutive years. He recruited boys to the Scripture Union clubs in the summer, often preached in chapel, and organised Sunday evening prayers.

Throughout these years, he never seemed to want to leave and seemed completely content in his role at the school, never restless. Successive headmasters judged him a superb right-hand man. Christopher Blount, however, recalled that David Cooper had in fact wanted to become headmaster and was disappointed when the governors passed him over. Despite this, his enthusiasm never waned. At the end of every holiday, he looked forward to the new term and to a new set of faces. He had time for everyone, and as dormitory master for some forty years, his kindness and steadiness reassured many an unsettled boy. He was touched to find a scrap of paper in Falmouth dormitory, stating: 'Mr Cooper is ACE.'

Cooper officially retired from Elstree in July 1996, with a dinner given for him at Boodle's, attended by guests including Field Marshal Lord Bramall, Sir John Parsons, Sebastian Faulks and several McMullens.

New classrooms and a recreation area, built at the cost of £475,000, were named after him, and his portrait by Basia Hamilton was placed in the entrance hall. Living nearby, he continued as a regular attendee of the school's church services, plays and matches, and ran a Bible class for the Year 8s until November 2009. It was through his stamina and interest that he mustered

David Cooper unveiling his leaving present

a large contingent of old boys, keeping in touch with them and playing golf with them when possible in the summer holidays. It is a testament to him that he had fifty godchildren. One old boy described him prosaically:

> One of the great indispensables, he made lonely and confused children feel that there was some point to prep school after all. People like him have vanished just as pink has vanished from the large, rolled maps of the world. He, and people like him, were the reason why the British Empire was the greatest Empire the world has ever known, and probably will ever know.

David Cooper died on 8 February 2010, aged eighty. A memorial service was held for him at Douai Abbey, which was widely attended by many generations.

* * * * *

The school had other memorable characters on the staff, including Miss Wilmott. Andrew Birkin remembered her oft-repeated line: 'One L and 2 T's – I like one lunch and two teas!' She used to help Mrs Sanderson organise an afternoon team to excavate the sunken garden, where the boys uncovered hidden footstones which led nowhere. Tim Christie recalled: 'I remember Miss Wilmott who taught us how to embroider, plus Miss Davies in charge of music (and rather frightening).' As for Miss Davies,* Ben Hay

---

* Miss Dorothy Davies (1894–1963) had been at the school since 1913.

remembered: 'Many of us were taught by the wonderful Miss Davies at a piano in her small bed sitting room.' Less popular was a man called Hobson. Tim Christie recalled:

> There was a terrifying master, called Mr Hobson, who was my form master in my second term. I once failed to state the imperfect of AMO, so he sent me to the Commander who gave me three strokes of the butter pat. The good news was that he was sacked at the end of that term (because I suspect that certain parents complained about him) and amazingly he then landed a job at a Midlands prep school where an old friend of mine was boarding. But he only lasted one term there.[22]

When lecturing to the boys, David Cooper enjoyed relating how some youths from London once ignited the science school (in 1978), and like many schoolmasters in retirement, he remembered with special affection the school's notable miscreants – in particular the antics of Andrew Birkin, author and brother of the famous Jane Birkin.

Andrew Birkin

Andrew Birkin, author of *The Lost Boys*, who arrived at the school in 1953, is remembered as a boy who was always in trouble. He recalled that it was not so much a case of him breaking the rules, but of him not

Andrew Birkin
with his family

114

being aware what the rules were. One time, at the beginning of the school holidays, he bet a friend a penny to jump on the track at Midgham station. The Commander popped him into the car, drove him back to the school, gave him three of the best and then drove him down to catch a later train.

Ian Sanderson had met his parents some years before he arrived. Although he thought well of his father ('very sound, farms at Chaddle-worth'), he was suspicious of the mother: 'wears heels, and paints herself,' he wrote disparagingly. He was clearly not aware that Andrew's mother was Judy Campbell, a well-known actress who had sung 'A Nightingale Sang in Berkeley Square' in 1940.

Andrew recalled the Commander as tall, angular and somewhat severe, with a dewdrop permanently at the end of his nose from November to March. He savoured the atmosphere of a bygone age. Outside the classroom, life was exciting, with so many forgotten buildings to explore, especially Home Farm, which at that time was unrestored and had not been touched for years. He liked the trees, the green spaces, and the lovely park they could run around in.

Despite Terrence McMullen, a later headmaster, telling him that he had been beaten more than any boy in the school, he did not recall much discipline: 'I do, however, vividly remember the dreaded report card, and the sinking, heart throbbing feeling that the sight of a third N.S. apposed thereon, procured – for one knew instantly that the result would be a queue outside the green baize door!' But he also remembered how the headmaster would listen to his 'woes of a Sunday evening in his study, and a large box of mint humbugs on his desk, into which he invited me to plunge my sticky paw whilst he patiently listened and advised.'[23] Andrew further recalled:

I didn't much like [Ted] Channer, and thought Hewitt a bully who enjoyed mocking me and others in front of the whole class. He called me 'Buku' because he said that's how I wrote the name 'Birkin', i.e running the 'ir' / 'in' together. Being generous, he probably didn't realise the suffering he inflicted.

As for Sanderson, I wrote to his wife Anne (in answer to a letter she'd written me about *The Lost Boys*) that HE was the Captain Hook of my childhood.[24]

Late News, 1958

The Commander enjoyed Andrew Birkin's school publication, *The Late News*, which came out every Sunday evening: 'This publication gave pleasure to its readers and, I think, to its writers too. Its commendations had to be earned. Its reproofs were friendly. No bitter springs fed its mirth.'[25]

There are other reminiscences from the 1950s.

Lord Fellowes

Robert Fellowes was at Elstree when King George VI died. Ian Sanderson took him aside to tell him privately as he was the only boy who actually knew the King, his father being land agent at Sandringham at the time. Robert Fellowes remembers the school as 'a homely place, a lovely house in a lovely park', and that a man called Dawson trained horses on the grounds. He was largely happy there, though when he was told he was due to be sent there, he prayed that his parents would not send him away and that his nanny would not die. Both happened. He recalled the headmaster as 'perpetually smiling, he looked benign. No one disliked him.'[26] He liked Mrs Sanderson, as she 'took the rough edges off Ian'. Sanderson beat his brother countless times and Robert himself twice. He thought David

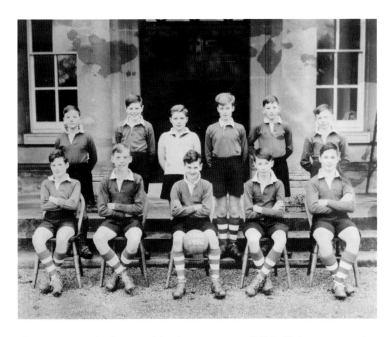

Robert Fellowes
(front row
second right)

Cooper was in love with the matron, O'Neill by name, though she married another master, Tom Raven.

Arriving at the beginning of each term by train at Midgham station, they would toil up the hill with their trunks on a trailer, pulled by an antediluvian tractor. Robert himself never learnt to swim at Elstree, but he was one of the leavers who clubbed together to pay for the swimming pool gates. He also noted that the films shown at the end of term were 'quite hot stuff', such as *Captain Blood* (1935).[27] Robert went on to be private secretary to The Queen, and later a life peer as Lord Fellowes.

Other distinguished old boys from this period include Sir Francis Richards (at Elstree 1954–8), who went on to serve in the Green Jackets and joined the Foreign

Elstree Midgham Station, 1958

117

Sir Robert Fellowes pictured with two contemporaries of yesteryear, Sir Francis Richards (centre), High Commissioner to Namibia and Brigadier Tony Ling (right), British Training Team Commander in Namibia during the Queen's State Visit to Namibia in October 1991

Office, eventually becoming director of GCHQ, Governor and Commander-in-Chief of Gibraltar, and chairman of the National Security Inspectorate. Sir John Parsons, who was Deputy Keeper of the Privy Purse from 1988 to 2002, was also there at the time. He went on to be chairman of the governors of the school. Mathew Pritchard (born in 1943), the only grandson of the crime writer Agatha Christie, was also a pupil.

John Parsons

Tim Christie

Tim Christie recalled that Ian Sanderson had a formula for dealing with prospective boys and parents. He would invite them to visit the school, but if he disapproved of them for any reason, he would simply tell them the school was full up, even if there was a vacancy:

> Despite the strictness of the regime, I believe that we were all quite happy at Elstree. I remember Mrs Sanderson's delight in pruning the roses in the rose walk below the main drive – and her taking me for extra lessons to improve my handwriting … She was pretty scary too.

A fairly extrovert boy – and good friend – of the same age as me called Peter Mavrogordato* was the chief moler for trapping moles who had dared to become residents of the First XI football pitch. Peter said that he needed to have an assistant, and fortunately chose me. So we were allowed to escape the morning walk to go mole-trapping. Happy days!

I was the only boy there in the autumn term of 1956 who took Common Entrance (to Radley), and the Commander allowed me to telephone my parents in the evening to tell them that I had passed the exam.

The next morning, the head said that I should go to the back door and await the arrival of Mr Hewitt in his green MG saloon (which he called his chariot – with a silent 't') to give him the news. He saw me standing there and I clearly remember him saying to me: 'Is it bad news, Jack?' (He called me Jack because a former master at Elstree was called Jack Christie). I replied: 'No, Sir, I have passed my Common Entrance.' He then said: 'Of course you have, Jack, I knew you would.' (Mmmmm ...! I wonder ...)

In the summer term of 1956 I was captain of the Second XI and we bowled out Hawtreys for nine runs. I got four wickets for four runs and James Wysard (a fast bowler and very big for his age, therefore highly daunting for the opposition) got six wickets for five runs. On that day the First XI won by seven wickets, so the Commander declared no homework that evening, which was excellent news.[28]

Another contemporary was Duncan Geddes. He read natural sciences at Magdalene College, Cambridge, moved to King's College and studied medicine at Westminster Hospital Medical School. He rose to become professor in respiratory medicine at the National Heart and Lung Institute, consultant physician at the Royal Brompton Hospital, and honorary consultant at the Royal Marsden Hospital. He is a world expert in respiratory medicine and cystic fibrosis.

* * * * *

* Peter Mavrogordato (born 1943), grandson of Professor John Mavrogordato (1882–1970), who was also at Elstree, was a King's Scholar at Eton and, amongst other achievements, the first translator of the Greek poet C.P. Cafavy.

Ted Channer in the Big School Room (now the School Library)

Ted Channer arrived at the school in 1953 and stayed until 1982. He had six years' service in the RAF and twelve years of teaching behind him. He taught virtually every subject, but most particularly middle-school maths, geography, scripture and history. His wife Molly was assistant matron for many years. In the field, he favoured football, and coached the First XI for many years. He was known for giving many a boy a good grounding in mathematics. He demanded neatness and accuracy at all times. Amongst his memories of Elstree was how unpopular the Sunday afternoon walk was, which usually took the route down the drive, up Cods Hill, round Douai Abbey and back to the school. He enjoyed the plays Mrs Sanderson staged in the hall in the Christmas term.

The McMullen children recalled how during lessons he would surreptitiously open his desk, obscuring himself from view, and dig into a packet of Refreshers, his favourite sweets.[29]

In 1974, Charles Riley was taught by him, recalling: 'Ted Channer was known as "Chanman". His first words to our first maths class were (and I quote verbatim): "You come in, you sit down, and you shut up!"'[30] In the 1960s, Mr Channer suffered a number of small heart attacks. He died in his chair, watching sport on the television in his flat in Thatcham on 7 June 1987, and thus missed invigilating Common Entrance the following Monday. As *Salvo* recorded: 'Messrs Templer and Argyle from Bradfield kindly came at short notice and took Mr Channer's place.'[31] Channer is remembered to this day by the annual Ted Channer Star Prize of a pen being presented to the pupil in each house with the most number of stars.

In the Lent term of 1956, Ian Sanderson fell ill and was taken to hospital. He was away for two terms, convalescing in Osborne House on the Isle of Wight, during which time Brian Hewitt acted as headmaster and Mrs

Brian Hewitt

Ted and Molly Channer with Brian Hewitt

Boys, 1958

Cricket practice, 1958

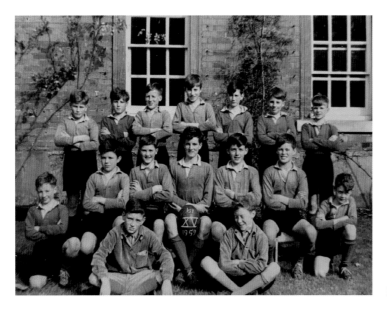

Rugby XV, 1959

Sanderson helped run the school. In order to maintain the impression to the boys that he was still there, his bedroom light was turned on night after night. Fortunately, he made a good recovery and was back running the school by the autumn term.

A house system was introduced in 1958 to give school life a more competitive edge. Stars and conduct marks were taken into account, as were inter-house matches and other competitions. Milky Ways were the normal prize, and at the end of term, the winning house got a half-day's holiday. The houses were given names with a levelling effect – North, South, East and West.

Nigel Saxby-Soffe (at Elstree 1958–63) found some letters the Commander had written to his parents, which revealed 'a witty side' to him. When at the school, he had been 'more usually in fear of his butter pat in the study'.[32] In these letters, the Commander wrote of how the stable clock, which had shown 10.25 since 1939, was now working again, prompting a gardener to exclaim: 'Old place beginning again to look like someone lives here.'[33]

Thirty-one boys went down with chickenpox over Christmas in 1958. When the boys came back to school in January 1959, twenty-two stayed at home ill, following which flu set in, keeping some sixty boys in bed. Only eight boys avoided it. Perhaps the greatest excitement of that term occurred on 5 March, the boys being kept indoors due to a rough and squally day. Suddenly, at 3 p.m., there was a tremendous bang, and a fine 70-foot fir tree was struck by lightning. The top snapped off, the tree splintered, and what remained of the trunk was split to the ground. The house and residents remained unharmed, but the power failed, telephone lines were down for two days and it took a week to clear.

CHAPTER FOURTEEN

THE 1960s

The school did not perhaps realise how lucky it was when the Bernard Sunley Charitable Foundation was set up in 1960. This was to prove more than beneficial to Elstree over many years. Bernard Sunley (1910–1964) had left school at the age of sixteen to embark on a life as an entrepreneur. He started out by hiring a horse and cart to move earth, went into the landscape business and became a property developer. An early commission was to relay the pitch at Highbury, home to Arsenal football club. He went on to explore open-cast mining and built over 100 airfields during the Second World War.

Despite having left school so young, he was convinced that a good education was a vital foundation to succeed in life. He found that Elstree was an excellent feeder school for Eton and Harrow, and sent his son John to board there between 1944 and 1949. John captained the football team. The Charitable Foundation has given substantial sums

Bernard and Mary Sunley

to many schools and colleges, including Ampleforth, Benenden, Gordonstoun, Harrow, St Catherine's College (Cambridge) and Magdalen College (Oxford). At Elstree, it made significant donations towards the funding of the outdoor swimming pool, the redecoration of Nelson dormitory, the science classrooms, the Bramall sports hall, the music rooms and, in 1970, a new cricket pavilion. Ben Hay noted: 'Bernard Sunley's support was crucial as was John's and James's subsequent generosity.'[*][34] The squash courts,

---

* John Sunley (1936–2011) was a governor of the school for many years. His son James, at Elstree from 1971 to 1975, became chairman of the governors in 2014.

The school swimming pool

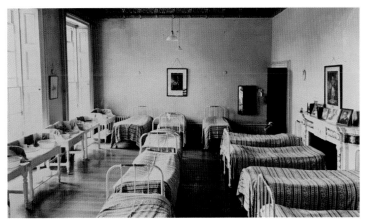

Nelson dormitory

First of the new
classrooms, 1972

Squash Club

opened in 1961, were given by Martin McLaren MP, in memory of his son Francis, who had died tragically in an attic fire at their Sonning home the year before.

Another significant development occurred in April 1961, when Ian Sanderson turned the school into a trust. Maurice Baldwin, a Harrow housemaster, was the first chairman. At that point, Alexander (Alick) Hay (1910–1984), who had been at Elstree as a boy, became a governor, serving as chairman of the governors between 1970 and 1974. Terrence McMullen credited him with having done 'a great deal to establish a thoroughly sound modus operandi in the business side of the school' and for having been 'a particularly wise and sound counsellor'.[35] Christopher Blount recalled the inspirational work undertaken by Christopher Parsons, 'a very great Chairman', who steered the school out of the serious financial problems besetting it in the 1970s.[*]

The handover was bound to be tricky after the school had been in the control of one family for 100 years. All too soon, a Labour government would come to power, stoking inflation and imposing heavy taxes on the rich. The whole concept of private education was called into question.

---

[*] Christopher Parsons and his son, Sir John, both served as governors for over twenty-five years.

126

For many years, Alick Hay had been running the family business, Naylor Benzon, which had close ties to the steel industry. He had a family connection to Elstree, too, being married to one of the Commander's youngest cousins, which further inspired confidence in him.

* * * * *

Sebastian Faulks,* the distinguished novelist, arrived in the summer term of 1961. He was the second son of Hon. P.R. Faulks, MC, a circuit judge, and the younger brother of Edward,† who was already at the school. Before he arrived, he was described as follows: 'Believed to be rather highly strung little boy, average at work. Destined for Tonbridge.'[36] Soon after his arrival, Ian Sanderson wrote to his parents:

> It didn't take Sebastian long to become an Elstree boy and I have nothing adverse to say of him and much that is good. His Latin is well reported on as being neat and accurate. Maths also accurate, not advanced, but a satisfactory standard, French, only a little, but will go ahead soon. English, well grounded, and promising all round. In behaviour he seems quite relaxed, most cooperative and friendly and his games are good … a very good beginning generally.[37]

Sebastian Faulks with David Cooper opening the new Cooper Classrooms

From Sebastian Faulks, an impression can be had of the school in his day, and the confusing atmosphere in which a new boy found himself:

---

* Sebastian Faulks (born 1953) is best-known for books such as *The Girl at the Lion d'Or* (1989), *Birdsong* (1993) and *Charlotte Gray* (1999).

† Edward Faulks (born 1950), a barrister, was made Baron Faulks in 2010, and served as a Minister of State at the Ministry of Justice (2014–16) and chairman of the Independent Press Standards Organisation from 2020.

Almost certainly there was tea, at long refectory tables with all 85 boys gathered chattering – tall boys, fat boys, dark boys, little boys, gingers, cowlicks and curlies, all with surnames, all of them bigger and wiser, knowing what came next while we four* looked about us, eyes wide, trying to stop the flood of the unknown. I remember nothing of the next few days, except a sense of falling and of waiting to hit the ground, both longing for it and fearing the impact. Every sensation was unfamiliar. Rough red blankets, iron beds, chamber pots beneath them, bells ringing, stern adult faces, enormous Miss Buddle with her bag-of-rugger-balls chest, old bald Mr Hewitt with his gold-rimmed glasses who had been there longest and carried the keys to the school's mysteries; plump Mrs Sanderson, now vanished after the treacherous Kim's game [a memory game played on the first day]; and the terrifying Head with his iron grey hair and his ship's captain discipline, a man who had instilled fear even into grown men at sea …

The trouble with Elstree was not that it was stricter or harder than home; the problem was that it bore no resemblance at all to life as I had known it. 'Have you learned the Collect yet? There's a test on Sunday after "Letters"'; 'A test? On a *Sunday*?' 'Yes.' 'What's "Letters"?' 'Writing to your mater and pater'. Lavatory paper that was hard and shiny, 'Now Wash Your Hands Please' printed on each sheet; porridge at breakfast and a strip of bacon served by 'simple' maids in overalls, out on parole, they said, from some institution even odder than our own; Wednesday half-holiday, morning 'buns', in fact a half-slice of bread with margarine and sugar; the Yard, the crazy paving, the Pineapple Gates; silent 'Collections' before lunch and tea to learn Latin grammar for tomorrow's test … The Reading by the Head of the School Rules, Rule One: 'Every boy must have a book to read, a game to play or be otherwise suitably employed' … Locker doors banging, a boy exclaiming, 'Landslide!' as his books and possessions slid from his over-crammed locker onto the floor; 'What's your occupation?' 'I don't know, I was just – ', 'You're on report. Go and report to Mr Hewitt'; a plastic washbasin set in a wooden stand, cold water in it, your tube of Signal

---

* The other new boys were Jonathan Halliday (born 1953), James Newcome (born 1953), later Bishop of Carlisle, and James Bagge DL (born 1952), High Sheriff of Norfolk (2017–18).

toothpaste, the only connection to home; Friday fish with bones and cold skin you have to eat; a conduct mark, two church services on Sunday and no games, but a walk in crocodile in grey herringbone cap and coat ... and the 'early boys' back to Number Five; too much rustling of the jacket of a book, 'Go and stand outside the Head's study', 'I was just turning a page, Miss Buddle', 'You were making a noise', and the wait to be beaten and the reprieve when the Head has still not returned by lights out; and a Methodist hymn in bed, 'Glad that I live am I, That the sky is blue, Glad for the country lanes, And the fall of dew. After the sun the rain, After the rain the sun, This is the way of life, Till the work be done'.[38]

It was important to find a way of navigating school life. Sebastian Faulks did so by working hard and earning stars, which led to the boys being given Milky Ways, and thus he became quietly popular. He was beaten twice by the Commander, including once for raiding the strawberry beds in a gang mission after swimming: 'The Head told the eight Strawberry Thieves to go and wait for an hour downstairs because if he beat us now we'd never sit down again. It was a long hour. The second time was for talking in the wrong place or perhaps the wrong time; but the beatings, administered with a "butter pat", something like a rectangular ping-pong bat, didn't hurt much.'[39]

Life at school improved as he rose through the classes, eventually becoming a prefect. He particularly relished Mrs Sanderson's scripture lessons. And at the end of the Christmas term, the carol services:

No excitement in my life had matched those evenings. I loved the readings and the music, but it was more than that. In the coming of Christmas, it was as though the world of Greek verbs, bony fish and grey shirts had been forced to join hands with a place of light and laughter – somewhere that in the long days of winter we sometimes found hard to believe still existed. The miraculous birth of the child had overcome even the iron naval discipline of Commander Sanderson; and after the religious hymns, the later carols – 'Torches, torches, run with torches! All the way to Bethlehem!' – expressed the yearning of small boys for liberation, home and coloured wrapping paper. I could never quite believe that in the school hall itself, the rows of benches crammed with excited faces and the choir installed in tiers up the huge oak staircase, that the day had finally come and that such emotions were allowed.[40]

Sebastian Faulks went on to win an open Benson Scholarship (worth £250 a year – half the fees), the top scholarship to Wellington, with an alpha plus in Latin. Commander Sanderson was waiting at the front door of the school to give him the news: 'You've won the top scholarship. Well done, Faulky. On Latin Unseen you took alpha plus which means …' This meant that he could ask the headmaster for a half-day's holiday. Lessons were cancelled and everyone could go outside to play: 'From being a figure of fear and dislike, I had become suddenly popular, especially with those I'd spared from a test in French irregular verbs. Out in the chilly afternoon, I strode among the grateful, smiling faces, trying to make it look as though this outcome was nothing less than I'd expected.'[41]

Sebastian Faulks remained loyal to the school, later serving as a governor during the headmastership of Syd Hill, and often visited the school to take part in literary endeavours.

James Bagge, a fellow new boy, was at the school from 1961 until 1965. He disliked the food, especially Marmite. He was beaten twice with a butter pat: once as part of the strawberry stealing adventure and once for forging the headmaster's signature (which, in fact, he had not done). He recalled matches every Wednesday and Saturday, and that if it was cold, they would try to get off games. Even if they did so, they would still have to go leaf-raking or do some other outdoor activity.

Charles Fox

Charles Fox was at the school between 1959 and 1964. Sport was not his forte, and so, during the autumn term, he often found himself on leaf-sweeping duty or cultivating his own pocket handkerchief 'boy's' garden. The joys of the grounds ignited his aesthetic sense. He recalled:

I gained some solace from the grounds: the rose garden, the sunken or Japanese garden, the park, its trees and the two ponds. At the edge of the smaller one there was a thatched summer house, behind which there was a tip, and a really good chance of seeing rats.

Then there was the long drive with two lodges and lined with Wellingtonias, not a bad walk if you managed to wriggle out of being selected for team sports. The short, or regularly used, drive was edged by an herbaceous border, at the back of which, at ground level, was a door measuring about 6" by 6". This was to provide access for a hose from the swimming pool to the house in the event of a fire. I appreciated the door's ingenuity, its position behind the red hot pokers, and its display of craftsmanship.

I also liked the kitchen garden, through which we would trot to church and back. In summer it was awash with peonies and in the autumn with chrysanthemums and Michaelmas daisies, of every pastel shade. But it also served another purpose. Apart from Sunday mornings, the kitchen garden (we were yawningly told at the beginning of term) was one of the areas out of bounds. This was not convenient to those of us who were on the edge of starvation. I cannot confess to being a paid-up gung-ho member of a gang, but as a younger brother I would tag on, something between a mascot and nuisance, and take part in raids to the fruit cage for raspberries, to the strawberry beds, and to the greenhouses for other delicacies. How we were not seen from the overlooking house and a phalanx of windows remains a mystery.

With our trophies wrapped up in knotted handkerchiefs and surreptitiously inserted into the tops of our gumboots, we headed off to a certain lime tree in the park. It had what might be called a crow's nest or a thick mat of old twigs and leaves about six feet above the ground, the ideal camp where we could hide, and where we could scoff our takings. We were not so adept at concealing our raspberry-stained gumboots which remained at the roots of the tree, much to the intrigue or at least one patrolling master.

Later in the afternoon, we squeezed through the barbed wire fence which prevented the cattle from slipping into the lake, and there on a tree stump overhanging the water got to work with a magnifying glass. Soon there were clouds of smoke …

Much more of a challenge than any of these trespasses was the lure of some dilapidated-looking sheds and barns at Home Farm. They asked to be explored, and one day we broke into a sort of mezzanine store containing a collection of goods and chattels. We were in heaven – until the ownership of this treasure trove became horribly apparent: a pale grey limousine came purring along … a divided windscreen at the front and an even smaller one at the back, and an elbow flowing over the passenger door. The alert was whispered, and having espied the headmaster fiddling with the padlock to his furniture store, Mrs Sanderson staring at we knew not what through a fiercely dark pair of sunglasses, and with the engine ticking, we ripped out some boards from a window on the other side of the building, descended a handy tree, and fled. Scratched knees and hands, and faces red with exertion, did not prevent us from sitting down to lunch as if we had passed an uneventful morning.

Looking back now, I am full of admiration for the Sandersons who not only managed a school – surely a big enough responsibility – but also ran an estate; and on the whole it was kept in impeccable condition. To me, it was a constant source of pleasure. Going through my ears eternally, much more than the sounds of cricket and tennis, is the sound of Atco mowers and tractors, and of the bells from church and clock tower much more than those rung for break or lesson. From the maids' rooms we could frequently hear, thumping away, the strains of Glenn Miller. From their windows they might have seen four or five boys slope off into the kitchen garden on a summer's afternoon.

I also remember an irascible master called Mr Baxter. He taught Latin. A handful of us enjoyed this subject so much that on Wednesday evenings we were allowed to meet in the masters' common room in order to compile cryptic crosswords in Latin, and to compose Latin verse. I subsequently found that this world of dactyls and spondees was streaks ahead of anything I was ever to learn even in my second year at public school: incontrovertible proof – hardly recognised today – that young children relish being thrown a challenge. (We also learnt by heart many of the classic epic poems.) I wish someone had told me then how useful Latin was going to become when in later years I came to qualify and practice as a garden designer.

Mr Baxter's temper was redeemed by stories, on the last day of term, from his days in the African bush. After much 'please Mr Baxter!' he would relent and his stories always began in the same way: 'Alright. Did I ever tell you the time our car broke down and we had to defend ourselves against a water buffalo? Now you must know that of all the animals in the African bush the most feared is the water buffalo …' (or lion or crocodile or hippo or whatever) …

Fishing Club

E. Hunt with motor mower

Staff prayer
meeting – Messrs
McMullen,
Templer, Channer,
Russell, Gardner,
Boyce

I am also indebted to the art teacher Miss Haig who turned up on Mondays in her Morris Minor convertible and encouraged me with what little talent I had as an artist. I now paint professionally, and thanks to lessons on English grammar and history have also written the odd book.

But most importantly of all, I am grateful to Mrs Sanderson who taught scripture, and who grounded us in the Christian faith, and to Commander Sanderson who led us every evening with 'Lighten our darkness, we beseech Thee, O Lord', a fitting prayer for a school whose motto is *Clarior Ex Obscuro*, although at the time I was too young to make that link or appreciate the values of either prayer or motto.[42]

During these years, a new science laboratory was built on the site of the present laundry, where the first lesson under Commander Watson was entitled: 'Science means knowledge'. On 7 December 1967, Air Commodore John Blount, Captain of the Queen's Flight, an old boy of the school, was killed. During a flight from Benson to Yeovil, the main rotor hub and blade detached due to fatigue failure of the drive shaft. It crashed into a field at Malthouse Farm, Brightwalton, a village in the Berkshire Downs, near Newbury.[*]

Commander Sanderson remained as headmaster until 1969. He enjoyed the idiosyncratic way in which boys described school life: 'We have just had our first school dance. It was against St Mary's.' He had his own way of expressing himself: 'I wonder how many boys remember how Canon Thornton named the three Christian ships. He called them *Worship*, *Friendship*, and *Stewardship*. Four ships make a squadron. I hope *Scholarship* will join after New Year.'[43]

On 18 April that year, 186 old boys (one of whom had left the school in 1899) attended a centenary dinner of the Elstree School Association at Quaglino's in London. There was a presentation by Alick Hay. The Commander retired to Lavenham. He remained a governor of the school and wrote his history of Elstree, completing it shortly before his death in 1979.

---

[*] After this accident, The Queen was never again allowed to fly in a single-engine aircraft.

CHAPTER FIFTEEN

TERRENCE McMULLEN
(1932–2004)

HEADMASTER 1969–95

'Today's demands require us to prepare a boy at the outset of his journey to manhood, giving him such armament as he will need against today's, and more importantly tomorrow's, tribulations. Our purpose is to evoke and uncover a child's God-given talents, and thereby to form his character. We aim to produce a boy of character at the end of his time at Elstree.'

Terrence McMullen speech, *Salvo 1992–93*

Terrence McMullen (1932–2004), sometimes known as 'Mr Mac' or 'BOD' (from teaching BODMAS [Brackets, Orders (powers/indices or roots), Division, Multiplication, Addition, Subtraction] in maths), arrived at Elstree as Ian Sanderson's deputy in 1968. He took over as headmaster the following year. When he died, *The Times* described him as 'one of the outstanding prep school headmasters of his generation ... remembered with affection and respect as a faithful, caring and diligent teacher

Terrence McMullen

and administrator.'[44] His motto in life was that only the best was acceptable, and he set high standards accordingly. His character was based on selflessness and integrity.

Prior to this, there had been concerns about the school's future. Revd John Eddison wrote: 'It was not surprising ... that as time went on we began to wonder how a school which owed so much to Ian and was stamped with

Anthony Thomas
and David Cooper

his personality would survive his departure.'[45] The school welcomed the
fact that Ian Sanderson remained as a governor of the school until 1974.
One day, Terrence McMullen arrived and David Cooper thought he was
looking for a school for his two boys, Mark and Jonathan (Jonnie). Cooper
was delighted to learn that in fact he was coming to teach there (and would
also go on to send his boys there).

When McMullen arrived, there were eighty-three boys, and the governors
immediately asked him to increase this to 120, which he did by taking on
some day boys. He appealed for funds for new buildings and introduced
some much-needed modernisation. By the time he retired, there were 175
boys.

He taught mathematics to the Common Entrance pupils, and scripture
to the young ones, largely to give them a firm spiritual base to their lives.
His approach was much praised by Peter LeRoy, former Vice-Chairman of
the Incorporated Association of Preparatory Schools:

> If proof were needed that a life of Christian integrity based on a personal
> commitment to Jesus Christ was attractive and compelling, then Terrence
> provided it. In contrast to the prevailing effort-based and moral exertion
> orthodoxy of much public school religion, he taught that Christian
> behaviour can only really flow from faith in Christ. He would calmly and

clearly explain the essence of the Gospel to young people, with delightful touches of humour and an engaging glint in his eye.[46]

One of his first actions was to introduce half-term, albeit only from Saturday lunchtime until Sunday evening. Until 1969, few dormitories had central heating. As related, the basins in those rooms were not plumbed, meaning bowls had to be filled and emptied by hand, and there were chamber pots under the boys' beds. In his first term, there was an attempt to improve the 'Gents', but Mr West, acting as plumber, forgot to replace the pipes, with unfortunate results.

During his tenure as headmaster, more classrooms were built, a new bathroom was installed, the changing room enlarged, a science laboratory and music school created, and the dining hall, kitchens and Sanderson Wing built. He also established Home Farm as a pre-prep school in 1993, starting with eight pupils, and reaching sixty boys and girls by the time he died. Mrs Micky Watson was the first headmistress.

Terrence Brian McMullen was born in Quetta, India, on 11 November 1932, the son of Colonel Denis McMullen, CBE, who was serving there in the British Army. The family returned to Britain in 1939, and Terrence became an exhibitioner at Cheltenham College. He did his national service in the Royal Engineers and then went up to Sidney Sussex College, Cambridge with a County Major Scholarship. He was a member of 131 Parachute Engineer Regiment in the Territorial Army from 1952 to 1967, and was awarded the Territorial Decoration.

He was an assistant master and later housemaster at Tonbridge School from 1955 to 1967. He then spent a year at Bramcote School, Scarborough, enabling him to become acquainted with prep schools before joining the team at Elstree in 1968. He served as bursar, head of mathematics and headmaster.

He was twice married. His first wife, whom he married in 1962, was Harriet Trentham, daughter of a naval captain. They had two sons, Mark and Jonnie, and two daughters, Rachel and Deborah. They all went to the school, Rachel being the first girl admitted (in 1975). Debs McMullen was a pupil between 1980 and 1986. She recalled:

To live the first twenty-one years of my life at Elstree was the most I could ever have wished for. Yes, there were sad times but the overriding feeling was one of happiness and gratefulness. I loved the community feel that Elstree created. Whether it was the twice-daily buns, the three sweets after lunch, the boiler suits, the much-dreaded cross-country runs in Park, Wednesday evening hobbies, end of term Convoy – I still haven't worked out the rules – the Ridgeway Walks, or maybe because I was one of the few girls in the school, I loved my days there. School matches were interesting as the opposition was

The McMullen family

never quite sure how to deal with a girl. Generally, they decided not to tackle us, which was an added bonus, although there was one match in which my sister Rachel struggled to get up quickly after a scrum and when hurried by the ref, she said that she couldn't as someone was standing on her hair!

The Common Room was always full of characters, and in the early days. Fiona Satow was a full-time teacher and my godmother. One day, during training for a major charity display, the rider kicked her horse, Budget, into a gallop and headed her for the nearest open space. This happened to be the First XI wicket. Early next morning, Fiona was busy filling in the divots. Some years later, Fiona used to take me for rides around the grounds on her Shetland pony, Bonny. I pestered her to be let off the steering-rein and after kicking Bonny on, we charged off and passed the front door just as Dad was waving off some prospective parents. We can't be sure if those parents sent their son to Elstree.[47]

Tragedy struck in the summer of 1974, when Jonnie McMullen (born 5 July 1966), the youngest son, was on a Thames cruiser party with school friends and fell into the river and drowned, aged seven. Forty-seven-year-old William Churchill, of Frilsham, Berkshire, attempted to rescue him and was also drowned.[48] David Cooper recalled it as the worst day of his life when he had to tell the school what had happened.

As this tragedy happened a few days before sports day, it was more than understandable that the McMullens were not up to attending. Terrence asked David Cooper to read out a message: 'Harriet and I are really very sorry indeed not to be with you today, but we are sure that you will understand our desire that our presence here following the sad events of the last few days should not in any way cast a cloud over an invariably happy occasion.'[49] David Cooper announced that the McMullens would be 'returning to full command next week'.[50]

The McMullens were divorced in 1987. Harriet remarried and settled in Devon. In 1990, Terrence married Mrs Margaret Whitlock, who had come to Elstree as school secretary, having been secretary to the Fellows of New College, Oxford. News of the headmaster's engagement was posted on the

Terrence McMullen marries Margaret Whitlock with Rev John Watson (left) Rev John Eddison and Rev Tim Sterry (right)

new common room board. She made him happy during his last years at Elstree and later in his retirement, 'easing his last days with her capable, unselfish, matter-of-fact care'.[51]

McMullen excelled as an administrator, masterminding three major building projects, supervising the wholesale refurbishment and extension of the school, and choosing good teachers, many of whom worked with him for twenty years. During his headmastership, Elstree was run with supreme efficiency. While he was there, the school won eighty-four scholarships and exhibitions, and about 500 boys passed Common Entrance, three-quarters of them going on to Eton, Radley, Harrow and Bradfield. By July 1995, there were 175 boys, ranging from the ages of three to thirteen.

McMullen inspired interest in black-and-white photography among the boys. In 1980, he and his wife took a sabbatical, visiting Israel and Austria. Mr Cooper was left in charge of the school. After the expansion and development in the 1970s, this year was one of consolidation, and with rising costs, the governors sought ways to reduce these. The home laundry was a help, and they took to letting the school out during the summer holidays.

CHAPTER SIXTEEN

THE 1970s

Anthony and Sue Thomas arrived in the autumn term of 1969. Early on, Mr Thomas asked a pupil: 'Boy, where is your extra work?' The answer came: 'Sir, the wind blew it away.' Anthony Thomas was born in 1941 in Whitchurch, near Andover. An only child, he was educated at Milbourne Lodge, near Hampton Court. He enjoyed cross-country running and was somewhat accident prone, chipping a tooth in a fall and breaking his nose by falling downstairs. At St John's, Leatherhead, he took A-Levels in French and Spanish, failing French first time around. He came to Elstree from Scait-cliffe 'because it was a nicer school'.[52] His interests ranged from collecting butterflies and moths, snorkelling, astronomy, skiing (which he started at the age of forty with David Cooper), mountain walking and athletics. It fell to him to test the strength of the ice on the lake to see if it was safe for ice-skating.

Anthony Thomas and his Astronomy Club gazing at Halley's Comet, 1986

141

Anthony Thomas skating

He taught French, and some said they could have passed their O Levels on the subject as soon as they arrived at their senior schools. He ran with the boys, he coached the first fifteen, took on athletics and ran sports day. He masterminded several musicals, notably *Oliver!*, *Smike*, *Treasure Island* and *My Fair Lady*. He also masterminded the shooting classes.

He stressed the need to concentrate 'or else'. It was said of him: 'He may appear fearsome to some younger boys but Anthony has a heart of gold.'

Shooting Team

There was an occasion during a lunchtime collection when the boys fell silent as he 'fired on all cylinders'. Following this, a prefect told the headmaster: 'I didn't catch exactly what he said, Sir, but I certainly knew what he meant.'

His first wife, Sue Cutts (formerly an under matron at Scaitcliffe) died of cancer in October 1990. She had ferried boys to and from airports, perfected the costumes for the school plays, and helped boys with extra reading and handwriting classes.* In 1995, he married Jeannine (Jeannie) Payne, who had been a sister at Elstree for fifteen years.

During his tenure, a chess club was created, and disconcerting school language was examined in an early edition of *Salvo*: 'D'you know, Jones is in the D, Binns is in Coll, Smith is in Gambo 5, Thompson is in the Book, Drake is in Yard and Morgan has gone across the Yard. I've just done a circuit, and I'm on a card.' During these

Anthony Thomas marries Jeannie Payne

Visit to Windsor with Colonel Dobbin, Military Knight of Windsor

---

* While at Scaitcliffe in 1964, I wrote a couple of quite long stories, which I used to read to the boys in the dormitory of which I was captain, in order to hold their attention and keep them relatively quiet. I showed them to Nurse Cutts and she was my first editor.

years, there were regular visits to Windsor Castle, where the boys were shown around by Lieutenant Colonel R.W. Dobbin, a Military Knight of Windsor, whose son Alec had been at Elstree. They were invariably sent home after a good tea served by the Colonel and his wife.

In the General Election of June 1970, six old boys from Elstree were elected to Parliament: Richard Body, James Dance, Sir Arthur Vere Harvey, David Howell, Stephen Hastings and Martin McLaren.

Humphrey Southern was at the school between 1969 and 1973. When he arrived, two dormitory ladies called Mary and Hilda started the school day by bringing 'hottish' water for their enamel washing bowls. The chief sport of the boys was to attempt to untie the bows on the ladies' overalls in the hope that their overalls would fall off. At this, a certain Hugh Graham was an expert. Hilda was of a certain age and at meal times would come up behind the boys with a teapot and whisper into their ears: 'Any more tea, *Maaster*?' Humphrey Southern found the lavatories without doors across the yard 'challenging to the gently-nurtured'; the bath hall, 'with its rows of monstrous tubs and concrete floor with precarious duckboards and open drains impresses itself upon my mind to this day'. During McMullen's time at the school, considerable improvements were made in these arrangements. Having shared the swimming pool with frogs and toads, the water having a 'green and slimy opacity', the boys were greatly relieved when this was

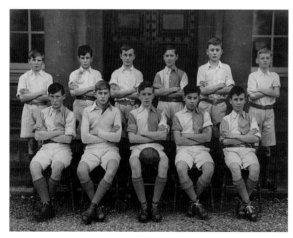

Humphrey Southern (front row left), 1942

Right Revd Humphrey Southern

The Kitchen
Garden, 1975

upgraded to 'sparkling blue waters' in a 'filtered and chlorinated pool'. For all that, Southern commented on how conscious he was of 'living in as beautiful a building and surroundings as I did in Woolhampton Park.'[53]

Inevitably, not everyone was happy at the school. Nick Vetch, who went on to found The Big Yellow Group, was one, while George Monbiot (at Elstree 1971–6), later a keen environmentalist, has written with disenchantment of his time there, critical of the impact the school had on him and by implication many others. He wrote of cold showers and early morning runs, adventure books being commended, other books confiscated as 'unsuitable'. He felt that being at the school had left him 'totally shut off from the rest of the world'.[54] Other boys take the line that Monbiot's comments were contrary to their own. The school remembers that Monbiot used to sneak out and make the mole traps ineffective at night.

The Monbiot Prize for Natural History is still a much sought-after prize to win at Prizegiving on Sports Day.

James Sunley, son of John, and grandson of Bernard, came to the school in 1971. His confidential report stated: 'He has done well, but is said to write poorly and he is in too much of a hurry. A big, well-developed boy who enjoys his games. Due for Harrow.' He went on to be chairman of the school governors from 2014.

James Sunley
(front row centre)

At that time, an amateur survey noted that most of the boys at the school lived in Berkshire, with nineteen in London, some in Hertfordshire, two in Devon, two in Scotland, and a few abroad. Swimming was the most popular sport, followed by tennis. Football was deemed more popular as a spectator sport, fifty-one preferring it to rugby, which got twenty-nine votes. Forty of the students holidayed in the British Isles, thirty-nine in Europe, three further abroad, and the rest at home. The average weekly pocket money was 10p, with sixteen receiving 5p and seven receiving 25p. Only one boy got more than £1.

Illness was a preoccupation of 1972. In the Lent term, the school closed for two weeks in February. Buildings and equipment were disinfected. Mattresses, pillows and toys were sterilised in Reading, and the gymnasium and fire doors were painted. In the summer, the boys suffered from flu, German measles and tonsilitis, so it was a 'rather mottled' term. In June, the whole school sat down for a meal together for the first time since November. This inspired a local garage owner to warn people to keep clear of 'that school up on the hill, which has a terrible plague of cholera'.[55] Another enlivening drama was when some black-and-white cows, a bull and an excitable horse were spotted stampeding around the garden area, the soft rain-soaked lawns, and up and down the banks, all led by the bull. They got as far as the grass tennis courts and cricket nets before being steered on to the meadows by Ted Prior.

146

The school has had a number of royal visits over the years. In 1972, the entire school went to Bucklebury to see The Queen drive along the Avenue after her visit to Newbury. A telegram was sent to Buckingham Palace wishing Her Majesty well on the occasion of her Silver Jubilee in 1977. Somewhat later, on 12 November 1990, the Duke of Gloucester opened the new Sanderson Wing, including a new dining room seating 170, dormitories and a dark room, a project costing nearly £1 million. He made an extensive tour of the school, met many boys engaged in different activities, and unveiled the plaque in the dining room. A special feature was a reunion with Mrs Florence Inman, who had been a nanny to the Sanderson children during the Second World War and had gone on to be his nanny in the late 1940s. Major John Henderson, the Lord Lieutenant,

The visit of
HRH The Duke of
Gloucester in 1990

147

Building the new Dining Room

wrote to Terrence McMullen to say how impressed the Duke had been with the facilities, adding: 'I am sure a lot of it would make Ludgrove very jealous!'[56] This was followed by a visit from his cousin, the Duke of Kent, in 1997.

The visit of HRH The Duke of Kent in 1997

Andrew Jackson died in a bicycling accident during the Easter holidays of 1973, when he was on the point of joining his brother William at Harrow. In the Christmas holidays, Colin Diamond died after one term. Presently, a teak table was given in Jonnie McMullen's memory and two chairs for Colin Diamond. Jim Champion and his wife Daisy finally retired shortly after. For thirty-seven years, Jim had undertaken every possible job – from window cleaning and caring for the boilers, not to mention regularly cleaning 100 pairs of boys' shoes, while Daisy helped to pack the boys' trunks.

Jim Champion

Other boys at Elstree in the 1970s included Francis Long, who remembered that Mr Watson (known in the school as 'Watair') lost their exam papers, evidently flushed down the loo by his four-year-old son.[57] Hereward Swallow recalled the letter-writing period on Sundays after church. The headmaster had stressed that amongst the many things the boys owed their parents was 'not least a good Sunday letter'. Some boys stuffed blank pages into envelopes, which may or may not have been welcomed by their parents. Swallow's technique was to write that nothing of significance had happened in the past week, in the hope that his parents would think, 'I must have obviously been working too hard to spare the time to either create news or write about it.'[58]

Alastair Farquhar (at Elstree 1974–9) went into the music business, working with the Bee Gees, Bjork, Ian Brown, the Cure and Van Morrison. He attributed his love of pop music to listening to it over and over on the school record player. His other school achievement was to notch up seventeen conduct marks in the same week. A contemporary was Charles Riley (at Elstree 1974–8), who recalled the foibles of some of the masters:

> Hugh Astley-Jones was a young teacher of Latin. For unexplained reasons, he only had half an index finger, which he delighted in waggling at boys in his class to indicate that they were to come to the front of the classroom. Another indication of his sense of humour was when a friend and I were bored on a Sunday afternoon, we went around asking masters what they would do if they caught us smoking (not a very sensible thing to do, and most took a dim view). However H A-J said he would throw a bucket of water over us![59]

Of Brian Hewitt he recalled: 'I remember he instilled "Mon, Ma, Mes, Son, Sa, Ses" into us by declining these pronouns in a sing-song voice. I went on to do a French degree.'[60]

A new bath house, a hard tennis court, and a new art room were commissioned around this time. In addition, a gym complex was started in September 1974 and took a year to complete. The new gym was to be used as an assembly hall, as well as for fencing, concerts, plays, film shows, etc. A new music practice room was also planned, along with enlarged changing rooms for the gym and showers. By February 1975, there was a new changing room, and every boy had his own locker. The new assembly

Gym hall construction, 1973   New changing rooms

Gym hall finished, 1974

150

hall and gym complex were completed by October 1975, and the school installed new gates so that people could enter by another route. These new buildings cost £127,000, most of the money coming from the Bernard Sunley Foundation.

In January 1976, illness struck again, with fifty boys down with flu. By special arrangement, Rachel McMullen and Julia Bennett joined the school in 1976 and were well accepted by the boys. Rachel loved the cellar and the wine cellar, especially when someone 'swung on the oil pipe and flooded it all'. She thought the food 'pretty terrible' but the activities 'excellent', and above all she liked the way the girls were 'welcomed into a man's world and accepted by nearly all the boys and staff as children and NOT just girls – this really taught me to try and look at people on the inside and NOT at outward appearances.'[61] After this, several daughters of masters were allowed to join the school with a friend as a companion, an arrangement that continued until the school went fully co-ed.

There was a change to the sporting calendar, with formal games on Thursday afternoons replaced by a variety of activities – anything from fencing, archery, printing, obstacle course construction, first-aid work, carpentry or handicrafts, allowing the boys great freedom of choice. Brian Hewitt retired at the end of July after fifty years on the staff, but would go on to become one of the school governors. Sidney 'Sid' Edwards, gardener and then butler at the school, well remembered for his kindness and patience, died on 9 July. He had been at Elstree for fifty years. The summer that followed was one of extreme drought, with baths and showers greatly restricted.

By the autumn term of 1977, the school had 141 boys, two girls, twelve full-time school teachers supporting the headmaster and his wife, along with four matrons, thirteen visiting staff, three gardeners, a carpenter, two cooks, and nineteen kitchen and domestic staff. The school had ten forms altogether, and a streaming system was introduced so that faster and slower boys could go at their own pace, moving to different streams if appropriate. The common room was moved to the prefects' room, now offices for some of the staff. The Big Schoolroom became the library, and senior boys' lockers were moved to the Long Room.

Cycling Club

Staff Hockey Team

School Choir

Roller skating

Golf Club

Old tennis court now Science Block

In 1978, the school announced the introduction of its own laundry, and an anonymous parent offered funds for heating the swimming pool. Around the same time, on the night of 4 August, two junior classrooms in the new classroom block were completely gutted by fire, causing £60,000 of damage. The boys were on holiday at the time, and fortuitously, Mr McMullen was still at the school and due to leave the following day. He was woken by the sound of a series of explosions. The fire was started by two young arsonists from the nearby Douai school camp. The police soon tracked them down, discovering that they had taken petrol from the school mower shed to start the blaze. Restoration work began quickly, but on returning to school, one pupil expressed his delight to Mr Cooper that there would clearly be no geography that term since his geography books had gone up in flames during the fire. His smile soon evaporated when he was informed that he would have to copy out all his notes again. Full use of the classrooms was completed by January 1980.

One week into the Lent term of 1979, news came of the death of Commander Ian Sanderson at Lavenham on 16 January, after a short and painful illness. A scholarship was established in his name to enable a boy to go through the school who could not otherwise afford to. At a memorial service for him, Brian Hewitt said: 'Ian Sanderson was in the best tradition of a schoolmaster, old-fashioned as to courtesy and consideration, but modern in outlook and toleration. His kindliness was unobtrusively bestowed on many but his high moral standards were there for all to see.'[62]

The weather being appalling that term, seventy-three boys lost a total of 180 school days between them.

The Frost Report on Britain (1966–7) contained a brilliant spoof on prep school headmasters, starring John Cleese, with lines such as 'I'd like to welcome four new members of staff this term, but I could only get two.' It is as well Cleese did not get his hands on *A Short Guide to Good Conduct*, produced by Terrence McMullen in 1979 and revised in 1982. This guide aimed to teach boys to behave in a law-abiding, considerate and sensible way, and made the valid point that any areas not covered could be filled in by applying common sense. There were imprecations to tell the truth, own up when asked to, avoid foul language and impure behaviour,* obey staff and prefects, work and play honestly, and to behave with consideration to others. It defined school boundaries and listed prohibited articles, which included guns, pistols, knives, matches, explosive devices, fireworks, radios, torches and mains-operated electrical equipment. It quoted Lord Tennyson: 'Manners are not idle, but the fruit of loyal nature and a noble mind'; on the matter of punctuality, it stated: 'Being late makes others wait.'[63]

At the end of reading this eminently sensible handbook, a boy must have wondered what he was allowed to do. It even told him when to go to the lavatory: 'Every boy should go "across the yard" daily so as to keep his digestive system in good working order. By far the best time for this is after breakfast.' Another line was clearly written from a position of experience, and said a lot without spelling it out: 'Some boys may find that they have to wash their feet very frequently, especially in the summer. Do not be lazy about this, as it is obvious to others.'[64]

Cricket caps

<hr />

* Terrence told the staff he would give them £10 if ever they heard him issue a swear word. No one ever did.

CHAPTER SEVENTEEN

THE 1980s

Steve Bates arrived at the school in the autumn term of 1980. In those days, he was 'Stephen Bates' and in charge of physical education. He recalled:

> I came on the cusp of the old-fashioned, no masters had been trained how to teach, and it was beginning to modernise. Nobody called anybody anything other than by their surnames – even in the Common Room. I do remember I had been here a term and a half, and David Cooper saw me at one break and said the headmaster told me to tell you to call him Terrence. I had to serve my time. David Cooper very much took me under his wing.
>
> Brian Hewitt had nicknames for all the boys. He wouldn't call them by their Christian names. When he was old, I would take him out for a walk. He'd come to church on Sunday mornings and say in a loud voice: 'Who's the lady with the terrible hat on?' Everyone remembers Ted Channer's packets of 'refresher sweets' that he kept hidden in his desk.
>
> What I love about the school is that it's changed and yet it's stayed the same, if that doesn't sound too Irish. The ethos hasn't changed. The ethos has been embedded in every change.[65]

There came an unusual day when the BBC were making a film about the early influences on Sebastian Faulks. Steve Bates's classroom was used, and the back of him could be seen as he wrote 'World War I' on the blackboard, the pupils acting as extras, dressed in the corduroy jackets of the time. Steve also remembered other school characters of note:

> Carpie looked after the boiler, the only person to know its workings, and he taught the boys woodwork. His wife did the laundry. Then there was Stan. Stan's room was the boot room. That's where he worked, and he lived downstairs as well, next to the boiler. He cleaned everybody's shoes. David Cooper would put his shoes outside his room, and in the morning, Stan

'Carpie' with the Douglas-Pennant twins

would have cleaned them. The pantry staff consisted of five ladies. They lived where the headmaster now lives. They were all a bit mad, but they were essential to the running of the school.[66]

By the Lent term of 1981, a new hard play area was ready, to be used for hockey and tennis. Elstree, like all private schools, was being threatened with the possible removal of charitable status and the imposition of VAT on fees, which would mean an immediate increase of £1,000 per annum. This and similar threats were never far away. The headmaster was concerned that the classrooms were becoming overcrowded and that there was a shortage of indoor playing areas for the junior boys.

Further classrooms were built in 1982; a new classroom block with six classrooms opened in the autumn. This meant that, for the first time since

New classrooms, 1982

156

the school moved to Woolhampton, there was no teaching in the main building. The headmaster's school room became a room for prefects, and Francis Templer's classroom became a library. The Sunley Science Centre came to life in 1983 with an electronics room, animal centre and reading room, and there was a new music school to which the grand piano from the front hall was moved. The old wooden classrooms were dismantled to cries of 'shame' from the old boys and rebuilt in the old drying yard. This work was largely due to the generosity of donors: Terrence McMullen wrote to Alick Hay, thanking him for a generous

Sunley Science Centre, 1983

covenant to the 1982 Appeal Fund, which then stood at £125,000, well on the way to the eventual target.[67] By the summer of 1983, the school had 159 pupils, 113 boarders, forty-two day boys and four day girls.

Richard Russell

In September 1983, Richard Russell arrived after twelve years as head-master of St George's School at Windsor, having just been appointed chief vision officer. Born in Malaya in 1935, he was a great-great-great-grandson of the poet Leigh Hunt (about whom he wrote a memoir in 1984[*]). When the Second World War began, he was sent to South Africa with his mother and siblings, where he heard that his father had been killed in the defence of Singapore. The following year, he came to Britain. He achieved an exhibition to Malvern College (where he was keen on sport and won the English verse prize). In 1954, Richard joined the Royal Armoured Corps and did

---

* *Leigh Hunt (1784–1859) and Some of His Contemporaries.*

Richard Russell
with Tim and
Henry Brierly

two years of national service with the 10th Royal Hussars. He went on to Pembroke College, Cambridge (where he took the English Literature Tripos and attended lectures by C.S. Lewis and F.R. Leavis), and taught Prince Charles at Cheam before going to Windsor. He married his wife Valerie and they had two children, Sarah and Anthony. He became headmaster of St George's School in 1971.

Aged forty-eight, he was happy to come and teach at Elstree without the administrative responsibilities of being a headmaster. He became head of the English department and took over the Common Entrance class in English from Francis Templer.* His aim was to help those in their last year at the school. He expected success from them, and resolved 'to take them as far as they wanted to go'.[68] He prided himself on being approachable to all, took an interest in the work of the pupils, how they related to each other and their families, and their sporting lives. His other interests included music, stamps, archery and photography, and he enjoyed his table at lunch, which became known for jokes and laughter. He ran the annual Declamations competition, the Kossoff story-telling prize and the Seymour-Davies Poetry Prize.

He took on the school library, edited *Salvo*, and in September 1987 he set up a popular school magazine called *The Pink*. It was so-called for

* Francis Templer died in 1990. His family gave many of his stamps to the Elstree stamp collection.

two reasons; it was one of the school's major colours, awarded for sport, and he had found some pink paper on which to print it. As he wrote in the first edition: 'It is the colour of health. It is the colour of perfection.'[69] *The Pink* listed school awards, appointments and news, and also had interesting editorials on wide-ranging subjects. It examined the origins of Christian names, celebrated famous men and contained many stories, particularly about Sir Lancelot. It was still going strong in 1994.

Richard Russell also wrote a number of plays for the school, one of which, *The Double*, was adapted from a version by his ancestor, Leigh Hunt. It was performed at Elstree on 14 March 1985, with twenty-one speaking parts. Debs McMullen took the leading female part, and Michael Tyrell played her husband, the actor Armyn. Many of these productions received enthusiastic reviews in the local paper.

He enjoyed sport and coached the under-9 football team until he was forced to stop due to hip trouble. He served as a lay steward at St George's Chapel, Windsor, and thanks to his invitation, the Dean of Windsor, Very Revd Patrick Mitchell, came to preach on 3 October 1993, describing Russell as 'your spy at Windsor'.[70]

Richard Russell retired to Bray in 1995 when Terrence McMullen stepped down, but continued to coach Elstree boys who needed extra help with Latin, French and English. His health declined and he entered a nursing home, where he died in July 2019.

* * * * *

By the autumn of 1983, Elstree had 163 boys and variously between two and six girls. On 14 November, there was a burglary at the school, which inspired some prize-winning short stories in the school. Much was taken, though the school retrieved some computers, a camera and a few cassette tapes. The culprits had broken into thirty schools, assisted by their research of *The Public and Preparatory Schools Year Book*, which they stole from a school near Windsor. Three men were convicted, with their leader, Bucktrout by name, imprisoned for two and a half years.

A pupil who was destined for international stardom arrived at Elstree in 1982. He was born as James Blount in 1974, and later changed his surname

James Blunt
study by
current pupils

James Blunt donation to
Elstree

to Blunt. His father was an army colonel, so his early life was peripatetic. As a child, he studied the violin and the piano, and was introduced to the electric guitar whilst at Harrow. After service in the Life Guards and in the 1999 Kosovo war, he left military service and shot to fame in 2004 with his album *Back to Bedlam*, most notably two singles, 'You're Beautiful' and 'Goodbye My Lover'. By 2013, he had sold over 20 million albums worldwide. Mr Cooper was said to be very impressed that one of his head choristers had found his way on to *Top of the Pops*. He married Sofia Wellesley, granddaughter of the 8th Duke of Wellington KG, in 2014.

In the autumn of 1983, James Blount took part in the school concert, singing treble in a Czech carol, and was commended for his 'very clear Rocking Carol to further lullaby-inducing flutes'.[71] In the school concert in the autumn of 1985, *Salvo* recorded: 'James Blount hammered the introduction to the theme from

James Blount and Cooking Hobby
(third from right back row)

the film *Chariots of Fire*, leaving us with some doubt as to whether the piano could still be in tune for the rest of the concert.'[72] In 1987, he took part in a production of *Treasure Island*, but was concussed on the first night. He was back playing 'an impish and endearing Jim Hawkins' the following night.[73]

There were many successful school plays at this time. Director of Music Anthony Russell and Anthony Thomas combined to produce *Oliver!*, one of a series of musicals. This was considered particularly successful, Anthony Russell calling it 'an entertainment, musical feast, and triumph':[74]

> Mr Thomas's production was superb. He marshalled enormous forces on stage at different times – no fewer than twenty-four bodies weaving and moving around the stage on one occasion – and this is a skill not given to all. He made excellent use of the front of the stage between scenes, ensuring that continuity was not lost, and allowing the greatest variety of imaginary venues. His attention to diction was most evident, and actors such as Sower-berry, Oliver and Fagin were easily audible, whether they were facing the audience or not. Brownlow's voice was another model of clarity, while Claypole ensured by other means that not a word of his was lost.[75]

In the summer of 1984, two more staff houses were built for extra teachers, followed in the autumn by further burglaries at the school. A total of 364 days of work and play were lost to chicken pox, laryngitis and flu. There were sixty-five boarders, thirty-seven day boys and some girls. In January 1985, the famous actor David Kossoff visited the school in the Lent term to read Bible stories. He came again in the early 1990s, arriving to the music of 'Bali Hai', and told the boys he wanted them to clear their minds. He encouraged them to imagine

David Kossoff

themselves looking out to sea and then back to the land, then losing their eyesight, and allowing the water and the land to become empty and black, with nothing in it that moved. He explained that this was the point at which God created the world. Yaltah Menuhin, sister of Yehudi, came to play the piano at the school, a performance much enjoyed despite, to the embarrassment of the school, one of the keys getting stuck.

The front hall was redecorated, and the Nelson dormitory acquired a fine chandelier. By the summer of 1986, there were 168 boys at the school, of whom 70 per cent were boarders, and some girls. They hit a record of 170 pupils for the first time in the history of the school the following year. That same year, 30,000 square metres of turf were laid to level the playing fields.

In 1989, Brian Hewitt died. Five years prior, he had become what one of the gardeners called 'an octogeranium'. Field Marshal Lord Bramall read one of the lessons at his memorial service.

Trampolining with Mr Bates

Gym, 1988

Orchestra practice with Anthony Russell in the old gym now McMullen Hall

CHAPTER EIGHTEEN

THE 1990s

Several leavers in 1990 contributed their stories to *The Pink*. Many recorded sporting and academic progress, but amongst the more memorable, Robert Figden announced that in his first term, he 'received an enormous black eye, caused by Edye, R.M.',[76] which Sister declared the biggest she had ever seen. Thomas McMullen (a second cousin once removed of the headmaster) announced proudly that he had received twenty-eight conduct marks in his first term, was kicked out of the under-9 football team for passing the ball into his own goalmouth, and lost his place in the under-11 cricket team by causing a run which lost the match. Luke Reeve wrote: 'Life for me at Elstree began back in the cold and frosty months of 1985. I was very shy and apprehensive. I was also rather stocky. I walked past a warm fire into the hall, and knew there was no turning back now.'[77] *Salvo* declared:

> To be a boarder is to have the freedom of being a boy among boys at all times of the day; it is learning to stand on one's own feet; it is the encouragement of decision-making; it is the discovery of the real meaning of home; it is the cementing of love for one's parents; it is the development of self-discipline; it nurtures an awareness of others … It is not the replacement of home-values, but the complement of them.
>
> Today's demands require us to prepare a boy at the outset of his journey to manhood, giving him such armament as he will need against today's, and more importantly tomorrow's, tribulations. Our purpose is to evoke and uncover a child's God-given talents, and thereby to form his character. We aim to produce a boy of character at the end of his time at Elstree, and in so doing we aim to produce what you want for your son.

By the end of 1992, the school was being hit by the recession. There were twenty fewer boys than the previous year and the annual income was down by over £100,000. No junior master was appointed. Terrence McMullen wrote to David Cooper: 'The books are just balancing. Fortunately it has not been necessary to reduce the number of permanent staff so far and I hope very much it will be possible to keep it like this, but I cannot make any promises.' He asked that costs should be reduced, 'saving where possible on lighting, heating and materials. If we all work together, I am sure we will get through these present difficulties and we will need patience and determination.'[78] In the summer of 1993, the headmaster said that it had not been easy to get new boys due to the economic situation. There were now only 106 boarders. Some had misgivings about boarding in general, although one boy had written: 'I tried terribly hard to be homesick, but I couldn't.'

Home Farm, the neighbouring pre-prep school, was created in 1993, with eight pupils and two staff. It took on both boys and girls, being designed to prepare the boys for life at Elstree. It focused on all-round development, building self-confidence and self-discipline. Terrence McMullen appointed Micky Watson, who had joined her husband Robin at Elstree

in 1986 and served as a junior form mistress, to be the first headmistress. Amongst the team was Sylvia Bates, who had married Steve Bates in 1982 when she was Sylvia Webster and a matron at Elstree.

It was not long before they were discussing two forms in each year group. By the time Micky Watson retired to Devon in 1999, Syd Hill had taken over as headmaster of Elstree.* There were sixty-three pupils and twelve members of the common room. Micky Watson would go on to say: 'If Terrence was my role model, then Syd is my inspiration.'[79]

At its creation, it was natural to make Home Farm co-educational,

Micky Watson and Sylvia Bates with Home Farm, 1994

---

* Micky Watson was followed by Sue Evans (1999–2009) and then Kay Markides (2009–19). The present head is Alice Bond.

as this meant it could attract twice as many pupils. Children used to come there at the age of three, but before long this threshold was lowered by six months, largely because as economic times became harder and school fees continued to increase, more mothers and fathers were out working. By 1994, matters had greatly improved, the headmaster reporting: 'It has been a time of remarkable expansion and progress, of cheerfulness and excellence, of true friendship and devotion to ideals.'[80]

Sue Evans, ever elegant, who followed on from Micky Watson, gave parents great confidence in the school as a happy and nurturing place for a child to begin their education. She took Home Farm to a new level, with new classrooms added and an increase in numbers. Following Sue, Kay Markides took over the reins and the school continued to develop. The Barn was refurbished, and the nursery moved to a larger classroom so that the early-years students (under Vikki Thornburrow) had the space needed to launch their educational journey. Later, Alice Bond took it to yet new heights, realising its full potential,

Sue Evans (right) and Sylvia Bates

Kay Markides

Vikki Thornburrow

Alice Bond

165

with pupil numbers rising from forty to ninety, by which time Elstree had gone fully co-educational. This was no mean achievement, especially given the inevitable problems caused by Covid. Home Farm's latest building extension is Sylvia's Barn, named after Sylvia Bates.

It was always sad when the life of an old boy from Elstree was cut short. On 14 April 1994, Major Harry Shapland (at Elstree 1973–79) was serving with the 1st Battalion, Irish Guards, when he was shot down by the US Air Force in error, in a UN helicopter in Iraq. He had settled in well at school in September 1973, captained football, tennis, squash and cross-country for the school's first teams, took part in *Oliver!* and *Christopher Columbus*, was senior prefect,

Harry Shapland

church warden and head of West house. He was described as having a fine personality – unusually charming, tremendously friendly, a great sense of fun and nonsense, and an unforgettable 'machine gun' laugh. He had found schoolwork tiresome, passed into Harrow on his second attempt, then passed into Sandhurst. He would go on to serve in Germany, Belize, Hong Kong, Zimbabwe, Northern Ireland, Berlin and Brunei. He was a competent officer, noted for his bravery, popular with fellow officers and men, and was awarded the Queen's Commendation for Brave Conduct for services in Northern Ireland. The Harry Shapland Adventure Play Fund was established in his memory, raising over £4,700 for play equipment for the younger boys at Elstree. It remains popular as an area for the younger children, and has recently been enlarged thanks to funding from the Friends of Elstree.

Nicky Montanaro had come to the school in 1988. He was killed when a tree landed on his head while on a CCF training afternoon at Seaford College on 17 March 1995. At the time, he had been sheltering from a freak storm. It was noted that he always preferred sport to the classroom, and had shone at rugby and athletics. He had won a sports scholarship to Seaford.

Ed Brims

Ed Brims

During these years, Edward Brims was a pupil at the school, and unlike his contemporaries, he kept a diary. Born in 1982, he was the son of Charles Brims, a newspaper businessman, and later High Sheriff of Berkshire and a governor of the school. The family had originally lived in Ramsdell, later moving to Brimpton Lodge. From these diaries we get an impression of life at Elstree between 1992 and 1996, by which time Terrence McMullen had retired and Syd Hill had become headmaster. Ed was a remarkable pupil, who has continued to be a credit to the school in his subsequent career. He won the fourth scholarship to Eton, and has taken part in *University Challenge* and *Mastermind* twice. Michael Hughes, his godfather, gave him a diary for Christmas in 1991. Ed was only nine at the time, but he recorded his experiences in this and two subsequent volumes. He returned to Elstree for the Lent term on 9 January 1992, entering 4C as head of form. He was made a computer room trainee and enjoyed hot dogs for tea. His diaries record the usual school activities – athletic runs, the winning of stars, hobbies and orchestra practice. With wry humour, he noted they played 'Land of soap and water (sometimes known as Land of Hope and Glory).' There was a lecture from a man 'whose leg was blown off by a booby trap. The man asked for two strong people and I was one of them', and the joy of an exeat: 'EXEAT!!! FREE AT LAST!!!' There were film nights: '*Treasures of the Snow* – Mr Cooper ordered *Tanglewoods Secret* but the wrong film came. Had to be shown over two nights', and a 'hunger lunch'. In March 1992, Form 5F were told to draw any item used in the First World War: 'I advised Bulmer to draw poison gas because it is INVISIBLE.' Ed clearly enjoyed it when things went wrong: 'There was a dress rehearsal for *Tom Sawer* [sic]. Dance's microphone was on and he went off stage. He said "Shit!" and because the microphone was on everyone heard him.' Mr Thomas terrified the computer supervisors by showing them the film *Arachnophobia*, in which spiders do away with numerous people in a community, and some miscreant stuck pencils through the pictures Nick Collet (1993) had prepared for his art scholarship: 'Today everyone had to write a letter saying how sorry he was about it'.

Ed also took an interest in the outside world, noting on 10 April: 'CONSERVATIVES WON. (but only by 10 votes [seats]!) – that is they beat Labour by 10 votes'; and after watching a documentary about Freddie Mercury he noted it was: '4 HOURS long'. In November, he noted the Windsor Castle fire: 'THE TREASURES ARE BURNT WHICH IS BAD IN A RESSESION [sic]', and later in the month the announcement that the Prince and Princess of Wales were separating.

In September, he became a boarder, which he enjoyed. Alex Berger stole his Walkman and Mr Cooper confiscated it. He celebrated his tenth birthday on 2 December: 'My Birthday! It was worth waiting for 1 year. I had a birthday table. Everyone in the school had a pong-wash to totally get rid of nits.' Jumping ahead a few years, in 1995, Ed noted:

> Last night I was horribly sick all over my bed. There is a bug going round. Bertie Kirwan and I have agreed there are actually two bugs. We had hot dogs for supper yesterday and I suddenly got a tummy ache while I was eating mine. It got worse and worse as I was laying in bed. Then I woke up in the middle of the night and was sick. I was sick twice more in Egypt. At 4.35 Mummy came and visited me and brought some books and my game boy. All I drank was water and all I ate was biscuits. I am STARVING. The bug is so bad that Chatham was evacuated yesterday to be turned into an extra Egypt.

This bug lasted between two and six days. Ed took the Eton scholarship in February, achieving 89 per cent, and got a distinction for playing the cornet in the service that Sunday: 'I am happy. I am very happy.' He was equally happy on 9 February: 'The barber came but I was able to escape from her evil clutches! She has never caught me!'

In May 1995, Mr McMullen told the maths class to take note of how beautiful the school grounds were: 'We then spent about the first five minutes of the lesson looking out of the window at the school. That is the best way to spend a Maths lesson!' Soon afterwards, the school focused on Victory in

Europe day, fifty years on, and then 'Mr Mac' retired. Twenty-seven helium balloons were released on sports day, and on 5 July, the school leavers indulged in a much-enjoyed school tradition of Leavers' Dares. 'Elstree RIP' was painted in white and a sign was inserted into Mr McMullen's home window: 'Headmaster for Sale.'*

* * * * *

With the end of the school year, Terrence McMullen retired and moved to a home near Chichester. In retirement, he worked for the Joint Educational Trust. In April 2004, his health began to fail; he developed jaundice and was told that there was a crop of secondary tumours on his liver. He died at home on 26 July that year, aged only seventy-one. In his local parish magazine, he wrote: 'I can honestly say that I have experienced extraordinary peace about the whole situation, and that I have no fear at all about the future, even if the endgame itself may be tiresome.' He attributed his confidence to his relationship with Christ.

He was survived by his second wife, Margaret, his son Mark, and two daughters, Rachel and Debs. He was buried next to his mother and son Jonnie in the churchyard at Woolhampton. Many tributes were paid to his compassion and humour, while Richard Waller wrote to Debs: 'If God were a car dealer, your Dad would be his Rolls Royce.'

---

* The only gripe Ed Brims ever entertained about the next headmaster, Syd Hill, was that he banned Leavers' Dares. It is more than understandable that he would not want to spend the first days of his summer holiday scraping red paint off the front door, or retrieving miscellaneous objects from the school roof. On 7 June 1996, Ed broke into capital letters in his diary: 'MR HILL HAS <u>BANNED</u> LEAVERS' DARES. THE ONE MAIN THING WE ALL LOOK FORWARD TO FOR OUR ENTIRE CAREERS. WE WANT MR McMULLEN BACK.'

CHAPTER NINETEEN

SYD HILL
(BORN 1948)
HEADMASTER 1995–2008

Syd Hill (born 1948) came to Elstree from Malvern. Before that he had been a Cambridge geography graduate, had captained the university's football team and won a 'blue' for tennis. He had married Jane Rust in 1975.

Syd and Jane Hill

Ed Brims noted that Syd Hill first came to lunch at the school in February 1995. Evidently, he preached a good sermon to the school on 26 February and in March came to watch the school play. Then on Sunday 2 August 1995, the Hills lunched with Ed's parents at home, and Syd Hill asked a number of questions about Elstree. That summer, he studied photographs of all the boys at the school. Impressively, he was able to greet them all by name at the beginning of the September term, and as he got to know them, often greeted them with a high-five when they arrived after the holidays. Thus he prepared himself for a successful thirteen-year stint as Elstree's headmaster.

His wife Jane had been a tremendous support to Syd when he was a housemaster at Malvern, and this support was continued at Elstree. 'We were a team and that was so important,'[81] recalled Syd. She was invariably to be found in the hall when parents arrived and left, and the author's son, Arthur Vickers, remembers the dog walks she arranged as a particularly happy feature in his Elstree life. When he retired, Syd particularly thanked Jane 'for giving 30 years of her life to supporting me in my profession. Jane has allowed me the indulgence of a way of life which I have loved and enjoyed and to which I know I have been quite well suited.'[82]

Syd Hill had been reluctant to come to Elstree at first as he had been so busy at Malvern, but he was keen to run his own ship, and he was persuaded by Rear Admiral Tim Bevan, chairman of the governors. He had never taught at a prep school before, but recalled that Terrence McMullen had been there for twenty-six years: 'A legendary figure and a breath of fresh air after the Sandersons.' McMullen handed over to Syd somewhat past the retirement age, and with the number of boys dropping from 170 to 134, Syd realised a new approach was needed.

The school advertised for a new headmaster, and there was finally a shortlist of three. Syd was even referee for one of them. They were all interviewed on separate days. One question each was asked was what they would do about the 'car park mafia' – the group of mothers pooling their ideas about how the school should be run. He replied: 'I would go down and join them.' He made a point of having himself or Jane or some member of staff in the hall at times when parents were there so that issues could be raised before they got out of hand.[83]

In his first headmaster's speech, he explained why he was sure he had made the right choice. Of course he thought it a beautiful place, with excellent facilities, but he continued:

> No, it is the boys who are so special about Elstree. They work hard and play hard, but best of all they look you in the eye, smile and talk. They quite obviously enjoy their work, their play and their friends. They achieve marvellous results in and out of the classroom but, and this is so important, they know right from wrong (even if, occasionally, like all boys, they need a reminder), and they are confident, open, honest and friendly in conversation. This is what so appealed to us when we first saw Elstree – the happiness and openness of the boys – and I hope it will always remain so.[84]

Syd was ably supported by Jane throughout his time at Elstree. Years later, when Terrence was dying, Jane Hill wrote to thank him for 'creating a school that I believe really does stand as a beacon. I know Syd feels that he has inherited a very special school and that he continues to guide it hopefully with your vision.'[85] The first thing Anthony Thomas urged Syd to do was to build the numbers up. By the autumn term of 1997 they were up to 180 pupils.

To Syd, the school needed 'loosening up'. But his modus operandi was not to rush in and make changes, but to listen: his motto was 'listen and delegate'. He had the ultimate responsibility, but he encouraged a pastoral side. He arranged for the scholarship class to contain two years of boys, so that the really clever boys had the chance to mix with the older year. They no longer posted exam scores, which he hoped would encourage self-esteem. He was glad that Elstree was a boys-only school, aware that girls grow up quicker and thus take all the parts in plays and music, whereas boys catch up later. He encouraged the development of Home Farm. They soon had between seventy and eighty pupils, and nearly all the boys came on to Elstree.

Syd introduced activities on Sundays, which had not been permitted before. He reduced the average age of the staff and introduced a tutoring system, each boy and girl having a tutor with whom they could relate. The form tutors became more involved with pupils and parents. One boy, Alexander Puxley, told his father he had had 'a smashing conversation' with his headmaster. His father said: 'You're not meant to have conversations with the Headmaster. He's meant to put the fear of God into you.'

He was keen for boys to look people in the eye and shake hands, and he enjoyed high-fives. He introduced flexi-boarding. Of the 180 pupils, some 130 did some kind of boarding.

During his time at Elstree, the school celebrated its 150th anniversary (in 1998). On a Saturday afternoon, they staged an *It's a Knockout* with sixteen teams, four from each house. There was a picnic tea in the back garden, and a

Syd Hill and family

marquee for an anniversary concert. On the Sunday, 200 old boys joined in, the oldest being John Irving, who had left the school in 1925. There was a cricket match, a lunch, tours of the school, and an anniversary service in the marquee with an address by Revd John Eddison on the hidden curriculum to be found in all good prep schools. He told the assembled company: 'The first element is to cultivate a sense of wonder, even of awe – the next is a sense of smell – the ability to discern clearly between right and wrong. The third is a sense of destiny.'

A champagne reception followed with Berry Bros champagne (Berry Bros were celebrating their 300th anniversary that year, and some of the family had been at the school), and picnics on the lawn, the Shelley Van Loen Palm Court string orchestra playing, and finally a tremendous firework display over the top lake. One of the guests was Mrs Kit Taylor, Ian Sanderson's sister, then aged ninety-nine.

Mrs Kit Taylor, aged 99

Four new classrooms were created, and there was substantial investment in IT equipment and a new design technology classroom. Syd gave an address:

> Boarding lies at the heart of the Elstree ethos and I believe very strongly that boys derive so much more from all that is on offer here by boarding. We see so many boys blossom when they are more fully involved in the School community. Elstree produces strong and healthy individuals because it is a strong and healthy community. As in many similar schools, boarding's many contributions to social value is the strength of the individual community it engenders. I think our Founders, and the Sanderson family in particular, would be pleased with what they saw at Elstree today.

During these years, *Salvo* became an annual publication, recording the academic achievements of each year over its 120–30 pages, including impressive scholarships, and the school's participation in sport, music, art and drama, all printed in full colour. One edition reported trips around Britain and abroad, lectures, book fairs, poetry performances, declamations, a European-language week, a Victorian morning, a World Book Day with

Horrible Histories, a maths challenge at St Gabriel's, a visit to Stowe for the prep school humanities competition, a day when the Year 8s took over teaching, and a French market. It explored boarding activities, a number of drama performances, concerts, art, DT, a rugby tour, a skiing trip, charitable enterprises, various tournaments involving families and old boys, the activities of the Friends of Elstree, achievements in the Elstree Award, fencing, team-building, and more besides. Home Farm had its own activities at a younger age, again with trips to zoos, farm parks, the Living Rainforest in Berkshire, Windsor Castle, and their sports day, drama and so on.

There were retirements and departures: David Cooper at the end of the summer of 1996, and the Thomases and Robin and Micky Watson in 1999.

Prue Matchwick[*] joined the school as financial secretary for three days a week in 1996, working with the bursar Tim Wynne until he retired and then for his successor, Charles Tibbits. She worked as Tibbits' assistant, looking after the financial side of the school until his sudden and untimely death in 2005. The chairman of the governors, Nick Bomford, promised Prue a locum bursar to step in as soon as possible – 'unless you want to have a go yourself?' She took the challenge on and enjoyed eleven wonderfully happy years in her dream job as Elstree's bursar, finally retiring in 2016. She worked with headmasters Syd Hill, Mark Sayer, Steve Bates and Sid Inglis, and during this time oversaw the completion of various projects, both large and small. The new science centre, Home Farm extension building and 'Bates' all-weather pitch in Budgett's

Prue Matchwick with Steve Bates, Andrew (Sid) Inglis and Syd Hill

Opening of Bates astro pitches

* Prue Matchwick (born 1951) was assistant bursar (1996–2005) and then bursar (2005–16).

field were the most ambitious as the school expanded and developed during the twenty years she was there.[86] Simon Attwood added:

> Prue tackled the fabric of the grounds, which had become slightly scruffy, grubby round the edges. When times were tough, she had a grip, one of the reasons why Elstree succeeded when other schools went by the way. She concentrated on the important things.[87]

On 9 March 2000, Field Marshal Lord Bramall opened the new sports hall, which had been named after him. The funds were raised by appeal, with special generosity from the Bernard Sunley Charitable Foundation.

An English oak tree, grown from seed from Sherwood Forest, was planted near the new hall. Rear Admiral Tim Bevan, chairman of the governors, welcomed Lord Bramall, 'as he had been a particularly keen and gifted sportsman at the old Elstree'.[88] Bramall still held the school's highest batting average, and spent the day of the opening batting against the First XI in the inner nets for half an hour, demonstrating 'that he had lost none of his cricketing prowess'.[89]

Rear Admiral Tim Bevan

New sports hall exterior

175

New sports hall interior

The hall was used for indoor cricket nets at the beginning of term, especially when the weather proved too bleak for outdoor cricket; it now hosts badminton, short tennis and basketball as well.

The Elstree Award was created that same year, somewhat based on the Duke of Edinburgh's Award scheme, focusing on service in the community. It was aimed at boys in their penultimate year and took four terms to complete. As it evolved, it addressed five challenges: giving a general interest talk on a personally chosen subject; helping younger boys at Elstree and Home Farm to read, including writing a book relevant to that level; helping coach junior boys at games; hosting the regular PALS visits; and taking part in a 24-hour camp that included survival and leadership skills.

On 1 December, the McMullen Hall was opened, featuring new staging, permanent display boards and carpeting. It had originally been built as a gym/hall twenty-five years earlier, over the boys' loos and across the main entrance drive to school. When the bathroom had been demolished, a vast underground cistern was discovered, so new baths, new loos, and a new drive had to be made before this building could be started. Terrence McMullen opened it, saying that it gave him enormous pleasure to have his name given to it. He said it would also give pleasure 'to the other seven living McMullens who have or have had close ties with Elstree'.[90] They then staged a performance of *Rock A-Round Robin*. At the summer concert, 'the audience sat in comfort, the lighting was atmospheric and the staging showed that we now have a remarkably flexible and user-friendly facility'.[91] Improvements were also made to the swimming pool area. In 2001, Syd Hill told the boys and parents:

> The final two years at a school such as Elstree are magical – a time when boys are old enough to make a significant contribution to the wellbeing of the community and yet young enough still to be enthusiastic about their school life: free, on the whole, from the pressures of adolescence and from the difficulties of being in a house and school with much older boys. It is also a time when boys have to face the serious responsibilities of their academic progress. The spiritual development is very significant at Elstree; the teaching of scripture and our daily acts of worship are designed to help the boys to understand the Bible and to make it relevant to our lives in this ever more complicated world. I am proud of the Christian tradition at Elstree and proud that it provides the solid foundation for all that we attempt to do. Boys will move on, quite rightly, to question their religious teaching in years to come but, more often than not, this will only lead to a confirmation of their faith and they will be eternally grateful for the seeds of a Christian life sown at preparatory school.[92]

In the following year, Syd Hill was able to announce fifteen award-winners in the Common Entrance exam. The previous year, 90 per cent of grades had been A–C, which then rose to 91 per cent. He spoke of self-esteem as a vital element in the boys' development: 'If you create self-esteem of the right sort in a young man, he will achieve his academic potential; destroy it and you destroy him as a person. Inculcating proper self-belief seems to me *the* single most important function of any decent educational system.'[93] He announced a new classroom block to be built soon.

The next year, Syd Hill paid tribute to ten years of Home Farm, describing it as a success story with very small classes, individual care and attention. He outlined the problems of running a school in the twenty-first century:

School teaching today is very different to when I started my career in 1971. Schoolteachers, like parents, do not have the moral authority today enjoyed by our parents and predecessors. As Bob Dylan so wisely predicted in the 1960s: 'Your old road is rapidly aging, for the times they are a-changing.'

Instead of moral authority, teachers have to take cover from the Children's Act, health and safety legislation, endless performance criteria and political correctness. This is what lies behind the dilemma faced by all schools. In an age of moral negotiation, nothing can be wrong, thus nothing can be right. If we hammer home the importance of restraint and self-control as the hallmark of a civilised society, our children are able to look over the school fence and see a reality where the Government and police send out mixed and confusing messages. So we are left with two choices: get out on the new road and retreat into Meldrew-like introspection or stand up for what we know instinctively to be right and risk ridicule and criticism from so-called liberal intellectual opinion.

The vast majority of parents send their children to schools like Elstree not because, whatever the media or the liberal left claim, they wish to purchase privilege and success for their children at the expense of the rest of society, but because they perceive that independence, even in the age of legislative constipation, gives us a chance of defining what is right and sticking to it. Like many other schools, Elstree was set up to reflect and defend those much maligned Christian values of public service, moral certainty and social decency. We owe it to the school and to you the parents, to ensure that those values permeate the challenges we face in the 21st century. Independence gives us the opportunity to be out of step with reality when it comes to the moral and social challenges facing our young teenagers in a society that is hopelessly confused about such things. Being out of step with reality may not be such a bad place to be in these circumstances. We will continue to stress the importance of self-control, self-discipline, good manners and service both in school and to the wider community in all that we do at

Elstree. With your support, and we never take that support for granted, we will do our best to ensure that Elstree boys will embark on the next stage of their education from a firm and unequivocal foundation, a foundation which will hold them in good stead for the rest of their lives.[94]

In 2003, an Independent Schools Council (ISC) inspection by the Independent Schools Inspectorate (ISI), concluded that Elstree had 'a distinctive, caring, family atmosphere that is very well managed and results in a happy learning environment for its pupils'.[95] A further inspection was made between 9 and 10 November 2009, after Syd retired. Words such as 'often excellent' and 'outstanding' peppered the final report: 'Pastoral care throughout the school is of high quality.'[96]

When Syd Hill retired in 2008, Steve Bates spoke of his considerable influence which had made Elstree 'what it is today'. He continued: 'His genuine concern for and the amount of time given to the boys have enabled them to develop as individuals, learning the values of respect and friendliness towards others through his example and without a hint of fear.'[97] Looking back on these years, Steve Bates recalled:

> Syd Hill was of a different generation than Terrence. For a young teacher Terrence was incredible. Terrence and David Cooper knew their roles and they didn't tread on each other's toes. Syd was gentler. He liked to give the impression that he didn't know what was happening, but he knew exactly. He had that air about him.[98]

Syd himself described his departure as 'a poignant moment.'[99]

CHAPTER TWENTY

MARK SAYER
(BORN 1966)

HEADMASTER 2008–12

Mark Sayer took over as headmaster in September 2008. He had
been educated at Tonbridge and
Fitzwilliam College, Cambridge,
taking an MA (Hons) in classics
and classical languages, literature
and linguistics. From 1995 until
2008, he was a teacher, coach and
latterly a housemaster at Welling-

Mark Sayer   Sarah Sayer

ton. He taught classics at the latter, and his wife Sarah taught in the modern
languages department. She went on to teach French to the junior boys at
Elstree.

During his time as headmaster, Mark Sayer prepared all the school's
policy documents for the previously mentioned ISI inspection, which the
school passed with flying colours. He led the church services with great
conviction. In 2011, the *Tatler Schools Guide* reported:

> There are cheery grins everywhere you look at this all-go, all-boys school.
> Something to do with the new caterers, perhaps – as any fool knows, small
> boys march on their stomachs. Or the sporting opportunities: boys represent
> the school, and the county, at a dozen different sports – football and cricket,
> but also less run-of-the-mill options such as judo, with three medal winners
> in the IAPS Judo Congress. Or the fact that the lower lake has been dredged
> and is now a paradise for canoeing and raft-building. Somehow they manage
> to fit in classroom time too, winning scholarships to top public schools – all

four boys who applied for music scholarships last year were awarded them. We hear great things about headmaster Mark Sayer and his wife Sarah – one observer describes them as a 'dream team', and Mr Sayer's PowerPoint presentations are renowned (or should we say notorious?).[100]

He was to the fore when it came to anything technical, and he prompted the school to have access to interactive whiteboards, as well as improving the use of intranet connections. He also launched the plan for the science building project.

Sayer presided over the packed memorial service for David Cooper, who died, aged eighty, on 8 February 2011. The service was held in Douai Abbey with numerous old boys attending, including Field Marshal Lord Bramall, Christopher Blount and Andrew Birkin. He was also very supportive when it came to the building of Alec's House.

Alec (Alexander Richard) Normand had died of a rare brain tumour on 27 January 2008, aged nine. His death was handled with great sensitivity by the school, with the friends from his year being told that Alec had suffered a lot but had now gone to a better place. Syd Hill described him as 'the archetypal Elstree boy'. His father, Christopher Normand, spoke at the packed memorial service for him at Douai Abbey, and his young brother Oliver played a moving guitar solo (the well-known tune from Beethoven's 9th Symphony). Alec's House was built in the grounds by Christopher (with

Alec Normand

Alec's House providing space for Gapper Fergus McKendrick to advise on choice of next school

help from many parents) as a quiet place for future Elstree boys. Next to it is a pizza oven, and many hours are spent there by both staff and pupils. In his valedictory speech in 2012, Oliver, head boy at the time (about to leave for Winchester with a scholarship), said: 'We in Year 8 are some of the last who knew him at Elstree and we will leave many of our memories behind when we move on. So it is good to know that this small memorial to him will be in good hands.'[101]

Mark and Sarah Sayer visited Korea and China in the Easter holidays of 2012. Later in the year, in September, Mark left Elstree and went on to be founding principal at the British Vietnamese International School in Hanoi, taking a binational curriculum for Vietnamese children between the ages of two and eighteen.

CHAPTER TWENTY-ONE

STEVE BATES
(BORN 1955)

ACTING HEADMASTER 2012–13

Steve Bates (born 1955) took on the role of acting headmaster, conducting the school through the interregnum year until the governors could find a new headmaster. He had arrived as PE master in 1980, and went on to teach almost every subject. He was head of maths and PE, a form tutor, coached every age group at every sport, including the First XI football team for an amazing thirty-four years, as well as the First XI cricket and First XV for rugby; he also preached in church, drove the minibus to any number of school events, picked up the Land's End to John O'Groats cyclists, arranged the Ridgeway Walks and travelled overseas to Kenya to visit the children's charity, Glad House. Alongside Anthony Thomas, he also ran in one of the London marathons. As Sid Inglis put it in his farewell speech, he became 'one of the great schoolmasters of all time who will be talked about in years to come in the same way as the much loved and respected David Cooper.'[102]

Steve and Sylvia Bates

His philosophy on football was that he wanted the boys to love playing. He stressed that the way in which the game was played was more important than winning, thus motivating the boys to high standards. He made it his business to arrive at school early and stay late, thus preparing places like the McMullen Hall for the day's events, and stacking the chairs when the day was over, not to mention disposing of random crisp packets.

183

Amongst his many other qualities were his patience and understanding, strengths that he drew on to help boys who were struggling to fit in or who were battling with their work. Under his quiet exterior, there lay a salutary sense of humour.

In January 2013, the new science centre was opened by Charles Brims, High Sheriff of Berkshire. Mr Bates balanced the role of preparing the boys as they headed towards the Common Entrance exam with participation in sport, aware that this allowed them to be seen in a different light. He admired the well-known Christian ethos of the school, and identified the particular quality of Elstree boys as having 'confidence without arrogance'.[103]

Steve Bates had never wanted to be headmaster himself, and was happy to return to his role as deputy head when Sid Inglis took over. Olivia Inglis

New science centre

New science centre opening with Chairman of Governors Sir John Parsons and Mr Charles Brims, High Sheriff of Berkshire

The new science schools

Steve Bates with
his first XI wearing
tribute shirts

recalled him saying to Sid: 'My favourite day as headmaster was when
I handed over to you.' She added: 'He was such a natural deputy head,
meticulous on operations. He knows the school inside out. He was the
dream deputy head to start with.'[104] Steve finally retired in 2016, though
he still helps with sports coaching, outreach events with local and private
schools, and the Elstree School Association.

CHAPTER TWENTY-TWO

ANDREW (SID) INGLIS
(BORN 1971)

HEADMASTER SEPTEMBER 2013–PRESENT

Kindness, humility and good manners should be the heartbeat of any school like ours.

Sid Inglis, 20 April 2018

Following a year in which Steve Bates had gamely held the fort, the governors appointed Sid Inglis as headmaster. Sid came to Elstree from Ludgrove where he had worked for seventeen years, the last five as joint headmaster. Then aged forty-one, he was keen to run his own school with Olivia. Born in 1971, the son of a Major in the 15th/19th The King's Royal Hussars, living in Brecon, he was educated at Radley and Newcastle University. He had taught English in Chile for two years before moving to Ludgrove to teach classics in 1995, where he became assistant headmaster in 2004 and joint headmaster in 2008.

While at Ludgrove, Sid had taken responsibility for the school's academic direction and the pastoral welfare of the boys, as well as advising parents and preparing the pupils for their future lives at public school. He led the Enrichment Programme and taught Common Entrance and scholarship Latin. He was keen on rugby and cricket, having coached the First XV at Ludgrove, and took numerous

The Inglis family

186

school ski trips. He also sang in the school choir. In 1999, he married Olivia Armitage, from Knaresborough, North Yorkshire. She achieved a first-class degree in modern languages at Durham University.

Sid first visited Elstree for a football match in 1994, when he was twenty-three. In pouring rain and a howling gale, Ludgrove's Third XI were playing, leading 3-0 at half-time. He urged the team not to lose it 4-3 – but they did. During the visit, he enjoyed a forty-minute chat with Syd Hill in the front hall, where there was a roaring fire and a nearby plate of sandwiches. As a result, he told his wife Olivia that if ever they left Ludgrove, he would love to work at Elstree. He has described his priorities for the school in his afterword. Of Olivia he said:

> Olivia and I run the school together. We see prospective parents together and give them an hour and a half tour. Each school day begins with a staff briefing in the common room. Meanwhile, Olivia is on the front steps, greeting every child into the school. She can scoop up little concerns quickly.[105]

Olivia works in the former headmaster's study. Today it is a place where the children are able to pop in for a chat, whereas in earlier days it was a place of trepidation. Olivia was brought up in Yorkshire and went to Queen Mary's School, then located at Duncombe Park, near Helmsley, where she relished 'all the childhood activities, riding and swimming in the river'. Following this, she attended Wycombe Abbey, which gave her 'academic rigour', before reading modern languages at Durham University, where she graduated in French and Spanish. She now teaches French to the top year. She has considerable experience in marketing, having worked for premium brands such as Veuve Clicquot, Red Bull and Boodles, and so takes care of the school's marketing, the website, social media and articles promoting the school (helped three days a week by Debs Burles,* Terrence McMullen's daughter, and Beth Davenport, wife of Francis Long, an old boy of the

---

* Debs McMullen writes: 'I have now made a full circle back to my father's old study, helping promote the school, while my son, Alfie, is somewhere on site enjoying his art or DT lesson. A dream come true. A recent highlight was winning the Old Boys race at Sports Day in 2022. I was given a generous handicap to match my age, and James Sunley kindly let me overtake him on the home straight. It is a great honour to be the first girl on the Cup.'

Olivia Inglis enjoying
a light-hearted
moment with pupils

school). She takes thousands of photographs, the best of which appear in *Salvo*.

Olivia also takes prospective parents and children around the school and prepares the pupils for their senior school interviews, later finding out what questions they were asked by the schools, which helps in the future. 'Sid's genuine knowledge of the senior schools is important,' she says. 'Values learnt here stand the children in good stead in their next schools. The children are kind. They want to contribute positively to their community.'[106] Olivia continued:

> It's all about the children at Elstree. We want to create a bank of happy memories. Ten years ago, we introduced Big Weekends, where we invite a whole year group to spend the weekend at Elstree, this boosts the boarding. It means that a day child can experience boarding from Saturday night till Sunday lunchtime, doing Socials and other fun activities, rather than the usual school work. The Year 7s might do a *Ready Steady Cook*, they might play laser tag. In the summer I organise a guest night: a dinner where all the Year 8s can invite a guest. We arrange the seating plan, carefully alternating children and guests along a long table. The guest can't be a parent. They could be a godparent, a grandparent, a family friend, a teacher, someone important to them, or a former pupil. We have drinks together; they take their guest on a tour round the school, before sitting down for dinner.

Simon and Sarah Attwood playing games with the boarders

Boarders' Corridor Cricket

Boarders' Brew, 2022

Boarders' Murder Mystery

All the new pupils come to our house for tea, and the Year 8s come for supper. These events are great fun and hugely popular. They also help children to be at ease with adults, which is important alongside the academic side.

Saturday school now starts in Year 5, which works well. When we arrived we changed the games kit to incorporate Elstree pink and navy. It was formerly red and blue.

Elstree has never had a tough, aggressive 'rugby culture'. There's always been a gentleness. It's always been 'cool' to enjoy art, act in plays, and sing in the choir. Culturally there's always been a wholesomeness, a grounded-ness and gentleness to the school. It's very much about the whole development of the child as a person.[107]

Sid Inglis is proud of the integration and performance of the pupils, their optimism and positivity, and the energy and the enthusiasm of the staff. He is happy if he looks out of his window to see children 'dashing off to fencing, tennis, extra work clinics, DT da Vincis'[108] or to find pupils reading quietly in the library. Reading is something he stresses as important, particularly as he senses the dangers – in school, as in every area of life – of a reliance on gadgets and social media, which he feels could lead to mental health issues. In messages to parents, the headmaster has expressed the hope that children will read for thirty minutes before going to bed, whether at home or at school. He has even had to berate certain parents who checked their emails during school concerts once their offspring had performed. In 2019, he tried out a 'Switch Off Fortnite', extending this to a 'Screen Free Saturday' and even a 'Wot no Wi-fi Wednesday'.

He clearly has a good rapport with his pupils, as he revealed in his sports day speech in 2014. He told the assembled parents and boys that he had asked the head boy, Douglas Wyrley-Birch, if he needed any help with a theme or some of the content for his speech. Douglas replied coolly: 'I think I'll be fine, Sir … How are you getting on with yours?'[109]

In May 2017, he consulted parents in a questionnaire as to how the school could be improved not only academically, but also with respect to extra-curricular activities. Later, he established a plan called 'Nurturing the

Pre-Prep children enjoying the wide expanse of grounds at Elstree

Chapel Choir, 2023

Future'* and adopted the Elstree Learner Profile as PRACTICE ('Pride – Resilience – Ask Questions – Craftsmanship – Teamwork – Improvement – Critical Thinking & Endeavour').[110] He has kept parents informed of staff changes, developments and improvements at the school, including a replica First World War trench dug in the camping field, a newly decorated dining hall, new 3D printers, and new Astroturf run-ups for outdoor cricket nets.

Recurring problems included the need to emphasise the importance of haircuts for the boys, and urging parents to drive carefully within the school grounds and on the relatively narrow roads outside. A more unusual one was when an escaped wolf was spotted roaming the grounds. After a snow day, one of the boys proclaimed that it had been his second-favourite day at school; the first was the day when the wolf came to Elstree.

One of his most important roles is preparing pupils for the transition to senior schools. Elstree sends boys to a wide range of different senior schools, including Eton, Radley, Winchester, Harrow, Sherborne, Bradfield, Marlborough, Wellington and St Edward's. They now send girls to these co-ed schools, as well as single-sex senior schools such as Downe House and St Mary's, Calne. With entry requirements forever changing, it is important to advise parents effectively and to match each pupil to the right school. For example, some schools offer 'unconditional places' (that is, not relying on Common Entrance), thus insuring against the possibility of a hiccup at the end of the summer term and a scramble to find a new school.

Sid Inglis particularly relishes the start of the new academic year:

> I always think this term combines all the good about the three terms: lovely late summer sunshine in September, conkers, blackberries and autumn colours in October and then the special post half-term build up to Christmas with the senior play, concerts and the Carol Service.[111]

An external achievement was to present a cheque for £103,000 he had raised for the charity Place2be, which gives counselling support to state primary schools. Sid galvanised twenty other prep school headmasters

---

* The latest 'Nurturing the Future' talk was held in the McMullen Hall on 13 January 2023, with governors, staff and eighty-five parents attending.

into joining him and taking part in a twenty-four-hour challenge that he organised in Pembrokeshire featuring kayaking, biking and running. He handed this cheque over at Surrey Square School in south London. This occurred at the beginning of 2020, a time when he was highlighting the battering the school had received from Storms Ciara and Dennis.

Soon after this, the school would face a greater challenge than drooping snowdrops and daffodils. In March 2020, the Covid pandemic forced the school to close its doors and to set up the Elstree remote teaching programme virtually overnight. It proved extraordinarily challenging but also energising to suddenly have to teach online. All lessons were live online and balanced with enriching experiences: tutors doing one-to-one online talks; the '*Casa Inglese*' evening in which Olivia and Sid demonstrated how to cook spaghetti bolognese; Joan Syckelmoore's art lessons (which proved so popular that she soon found she had parents keen to take part). Mary Westley's interactive Zoom music lessons also became a real hit. There were lots of athletic challenges too.

The school itself retained a strong number of resident staff, who waved at each other from the requisite distance. They arranged quizzes and would all come out on Thursday evenings to clap for the NHS. The ongoing closure of the school necessitated the introduction of surface devices for Years 6, 7 and 8. Although everyone communicated regularly, inevitably the older members of staff were less inclined towards technology, but this gave the younger ones the chance to guide them through the world of Zoom lessons and PowerPoints. The result was that it brought the school community much closer. Moreover, the new forms of technology led to greater efficiency. Olivia Inglis recalled:

> Covid was incredibly challenging, with huge worries about the children not being here, and for their mental health. Doing all lessons on a screen, particularly for the younger ones, was really difficult. Lessons were on Teams and preparation for them was intense. Academically, my French set made more progress because the lessons were so focused. You had a whole hour. No one ever missed it for a music practice or a play rehearsal, but what they really missed was friends, sport, choir, boarding.

Ice Bucket Challenge. Sid Inglis and Steve Bates, 2014

Lacrosse

Football

Rugby

Kayaking and canoeing

Netball

Showjumping

Sid and I did a cook along, a *Casa Inglese*. We had 120 families on Zoom cooking along with us in their kitchens, and we did mass school quizzes with all the parents, a fitness programme, and an internal quiz for the staff. Additionally, there were financial worries. We had to reduce fees and staff had to be furloughed. It was a really stressful time.

When the children eventually returned to school, we had to test the Year 7s and 8s regularly for Covid and they wore masks. We had a one-way system round the school. Life was really structured and restricted for the children but they were so accepting, it was better than home learning. In 2020 we held our Easter service early just before lockdown when the children were sent home. And in 2021 the carol service was held outside.[112]

As a direct result of Covid, there was a mass exodus of families from London, as some parents found they could work more flexibly from home. As Sid put it: 'When the restrictions relaxed, the touchline on a Wednesday was heaving!' On the other hand, full boarding shrank somewhat and there were fewer pupils from overseas. The school became more locally orientated, and flexi-boarding flourished, the benefit being that every pupil who boarded did so because it was what they wanted.

The second, more exciting challenge was the school going fully co-educational, arguably the most significant development in the entire history of Elstree (other than the move to Woolhampton). This idea had been resisted in the past, partly on the grounds that girls were thought to develop more quickly than boys and that boys arguably worked better in an all-male environment. But as so often happens, times change, and the move to fully co-educational was deemed 'a resounding success'. Although Home Farm had always been co-ed, on reaching Year 2, the boys could come to Elstree, but the girls had to go elsewhere. In September 2020, thirty-one girls started at Elstree, of whom fourteen had been in the pre-prep school. Six more girls joined in the Lent term of 2021, and a further four in the summer term. Olivia Inglis explained:

> The move to co-education has been incredibly exciting and positive. Originally, girls were going to be introduced gradually from the pre-prep, but a lot of the girls who had been at the pre-prep and then gone elsewhere returned

Girls in the school, 2022

to Elstree when we made the move to co-education. A lot of older sisters made the move to Elstree. Some families with three boys at home welcomed it as they had no sisters at home. Girl numbers soon rose to 62, then 84. By September 2023 we will have over 100 girls, which is really exciting and incredibly energising. The first girls were called the pioneer girls. We had put plenty of time and thought into the planning for co-education, and there was little negative reaction when it was announced. On the contrary, everyone was incredibly positive. We enjoy looking after children, treating boys and girls as individuals, whilst keeping the class sizes small, which helps.[113]

To accommodate the girls, several areas of the school had to be redeveloped. Sandersons was converted to a girls' wing, with girls' dormitories named after inspirational women, such as Thatcher, Seacole and Finlay, the latter named after a particularly popular school sister. Hockey was adopted for the Autumn Term, netball during Lent, and the girls participated in cross-country and some football, along with athletics, swimming and even co-ed cricket in the summer. A head of girls, Mrs Crispy Kidson, was appointed, and a head of girls' games, Mrs Katie Sanford.

Making the most of life at Elstree

The arrival of the girls was said to have brought 'a wave of enthusiasm and a real sense of purpose with them.'[114] Presently, the boy-girl ratio in Year 3 is 50:50. The girls are thriving at Elstree. There are brothers and sisters, but sometimes parents want to send their boys to Elstree simply for the presence of girls, a bit of female influence. At the same time, numbers at Home Farm (now known as Elstree Pre-Prep) doubled. Steve Bates commented: 'The ease with which Elstree has gone co-ed is remarkable, which is all down to the leadership of Sid and Olivia.'[115]

By 2022, there were 270 pupils, with 180 of them in the prep school from Year 3 to Year 8. Sid Inglis has no plans to move on:

> When we took over, we were told that Elstree had lost a bit of its soul, its spirit, and it just needed a bit of love. Numbers had dipped, and we had to fight harder for children, but now strangely a combination of Covid, an exodus of families from London and a new head of Pre-Prep – Alice Bond – things are flourishing. After ten years we have no plans to go anywhere. We want this to be our legacy.
>
> There's a gentleness and a strong Christian ethos at the school. Christian values are taught and celebrated. We want children to think it is cool to work hard and to read, to enjoy art and drama and not to think that it is only cool to take part in sport. We try to promote the importance of getting the small things right. The idea that if you are in work mode, make that your priority. If you are coming into church, then show some deference to the situation and look smart. Then, when the bell goes for break time, you run around, and create plenty of happy noise and chatter.[116]

Olivia introduced the Manners Challenges – a weekly challenge focusing on table manners, etiquette and general manners. Sid sings in the choir alongside his deputy head, Simon Attwood, and other members of staff. To this, Olivia added: 'Sid loves leading the church services, the whole school being together. The Saturday service is his favourite time of the week.'[117]

In the summer of 2022, the school was able to enjoy a full and traditional summer term, made more special by their celebrations to mark the Queen's Platinum Jubilee. Two hundred took part, including past pupils, parents, staff and governors. There was a '*Diner en Rouge, Blanc et Bleu*',

The Queen's Platinum Jubilee 2022 'Diner en Rouge, Blanc et Bleu'

The Queen's Platinum Jubilee, 2022

The Queen's Platinum Jubilee Tea and concert and tapestry

The Queen's Platinum Jubilee Tea and concert

The Queen's Platinum Jubilee Jamboree, 2022

which was essentially a bring-your-own pop-up picnic. The next day, everyone came dressed in red, white and blue for the Jubilee Jamboree with every possible kind of riotous fun. Later, there was a tea and prep-school concert, an array of cakes and a glass of fizz to toast The Queen. The national anthem was sung, and 'The White Cliffs of Dover' ended the evening with joy and pride and a few tears of emotion.

The Queen's Platinum Jubilee Dog Show

The Queen's Platinum Jubilee Toddler Group

The Queen's Platinum Jubilee Bake-off.
Bobby and Carrie Blackwell

The Queen's Platinum Jubilee Pre-Prep
Guardsmen

The Queen's Platinum Jubilee Garden

The Queen's Platinum Jubilee Tapestry

All pupils contributed a square to the Platinum Jubilee tapestry that now hangs in the front hall. Since the spring, the children had worked with Mrs Syckelmoore to bring the Platinum Jubilee Garden to life, 'in honour of The Queen.'

The autumn term began on 7 September. A day later came the announcement that The Queen had died at Balmoral at the age of ninety-six, after a reign of over seventy years. Sid Inglis said:

> It was a hugely unifying time for us all and Her Majesty's qualities always gave us themes to focus on at the beginning of the year. We celebrated her commitment, service, respect, loyalty, and steadfastness. We held a special Act of Remembrance at the front of the school, with prep and pre-prep children and staff, as well as wider staff, all paying their respects. In addition, we have had two memorable church services in St Peter's, with flocks of parents also joining us at our services.[118]

CHAPTER TWENTY-THREE

EPILOGUE

2023 marks Elstree's 175-year anniversary as a school. It is interesting to look back at a photograph of the masters at Elstree Hill in 1876. They were a motley crew, dressed in a variety of clothes – from Monsieur Pingon in a dark frock coat and tall silk hat, to men in light suits and boaters, or white bowler hats. Variously, they sported beards, whiskers and drooping moustaches.

Times have changed considerably since those far-off days when a host of young Sandersons were to be seen drifting about the grounds, and figures like John Galsworthy or

Staff, 1870

Commander Sanderson and Staff, 1968 (including Messrs Cooper, Hewitt and Channer)

Staff, 1970s

Joseph Conrad came to visit the headmaster and his family. They were sterner men, no doubt, and their approach to education was likewise stricter and more severe. Yet surely they would be pleased to see the school flourishing in beautiful grounds, the youngsters happy to be there, the school competing well with its rivals. They might shake their heads, perhaps, at the thought that the boys were nurtured and encouraged rather than kept in an atmosphere of fear, at times of terror. Mercifully, those days are long over.

Teaching staff, 2023

Administrative staff, 2023

In his 2019 sports day speech, Sid Inglis mused on what Commander Sanderson might think of the present-day Elstree. He thought he would be proud:

> He would love the fact that the park and gardens are used so widely, he would rejoice in all the activities that the children so enjoy, he would admire

Pre-Prep staff, 2023

the rigour and ambition of classroom life, but thoroughly approve of the aim of developing children who are polite, full of respect and humility and integrity, who value the importance of doing something to the best of their ability and, most importantly, understanding that kindness and compassion should be the absolute basis for how we behave and look after others.[119]

And those old schoolmasters of yesteryear would surely commend Elstree for continuing to send young men – and now young women – out into the world with a good grounding and a Christian ethical approach to life. For what runs through the whole history of the school is that it is not just a matter of 'driving boys down a corridor with a sign saying Common Entrance at the end of it',[120] but giving them a strong moral compass for life, and to be good citizens in the world that awaits them outside the school's gates.

As one school sermon put it, life could be 'wonderful' or it could be 'blunderful', but the pupils must keep a firm eye on the future – and be 'yonderful'.

Old Boys and Girl with current children in the school, Oct 2021

THE FUTURE
Sid Inglis

Reading the chapters which chart the history of this wonderful school, I cannot help but be humbled and privileged to follow some of the great Headmasters of their generations. There is an aura surrounding the names of Sanderson, Bernays, McMullen and Hill, and I hope that they would be as proud of the Elstree today as they were when they held the reins of the school. As we mark Elstree's 175th anniversary, we want to absorb the history, traditions and achievements of the school and, in turn, look ahead to what the Elstree of the 21st century will continue to look like. It is said that a great school is one that maintains its relevance and place in an ever-changing world, and Elstree should be no exception.

As a very community-centric school, with a real emphasis on the importance of family life, the move to full co-education in September 2020 became a natural and hugely positive development, arguably the most significant strategic move in the school's history, since the transition to Woolhampton in 1939. Families were looking for a school where both boys and girls could be celebrated and nurtured. Parents often commented that, in Elstree, they had found the perfect school for their son, but could not find the same for their daughter. With boys and girls now able to enjoy everything that an Elstree education has to offer, the school has maintained its purpose, and adapted to a world in which men and women, rightly, are given equal opportunities to flourish.

Elstree provides an environment where both boys and girls can develop the skills necessary to thrive in the modern world. The ethos and values remain unchanged. We are so proud of our rich history and reputation as a school with high academic, creative and sporting aspirations. We want children to aim high and to be the best possible version of themselves, but to keep their feet firmly on the ground. There is a straightforwardness to the school's approach that allows the pupils to develop at their own pace and in their own way. Whilst we recognise that success is something to celebrate, we believe that being open, compassionate and tolerant of others is equally important. Our boys and girls lead fulfilling and purposeful lives, benefitting from an all-round education based on Christian values and a strong sense of community, where kindness, compassion, ambition and endeavour are daily watchwords.

As one parent concluded:

> We chose Elstree as a school for our children because we were so taken with the values and educational philosophy of the Headmaster and his wife. We really liked the fact that they weren't afraid to be ambitious for the pupils – some country prep schools can be a bit apologetic about this – whilst always maintaining a warm, secure and encouraging environment.
>
> Impeccable manners, humility, intellectual curiosity, a sense of purpose, the importance of community, the value of hard work and an appreciation of the sheer fun and adventure that life has to offer, permeate the school. No matter where a child sits academically, it is a lasting gift to have been immersed in such a culture and to carry this set of principles forward in life.

It is now almost 10 years since Olivia and I, and our three children, Eliza, Johnny and Tom, joined the Elstree community, and, leading the school together, we have made it our mission to nurture an ethos of family-values and an emphasis on kindness, ambition and making the most of opportunities. We have been blessed with the support of a hugely talented staff team and an equally committed Governing body,

Sid and Olivia Inglis

led by the indefatigable James Sunley. All members of the Elstree 'crew' contribute in so many ways to the happy and purposeful atmosphere. The emphasis on high standards and doing the small things thoroughly well, is something that all members of the school community embrace. Their efforts to navigate their way through the gruelling times of the Covid pandemic

Prizegiving in the Covid-19 era

were truly outstanding, and real evidence of the marvellous Elstree team spirit.

Now that this extraordinary period has passed, we can look back with such pride at how the school community rallied together; it was a strangely energising and rewarding time. There is nothing in the 'How to be a good Headmaster' manual that teaches you how to manage a school during a global pandemic, and I remain truly grateful for the support of the staff, parents, pupils and Governors. Not only did we offer a gold-plated remote teaching and learning programme, with staff delivering live online lessons with canva quizzes, break out rooms and Quizlet-live games, but we also managed to engage the boys and girls (and their families) with many, albethey remote, co-curricular activities and events, from the *Casa Inglese* 'Cookalong' evening, the whole school 'Jerusalema' dance, on-line HIIT sessions, family Art classes and the live-streamed Elstree Big Quiz.

Despite the frequently documented challenges that face young people today, I maintain that there is still a blissful simplicity to childhood that all schools should work hard to retain. One only needs to recall the memorable 'Snow Day' in 2018 when only half the pupils were able to travel to Elstree. Simon Attwood, Elstree's ever-resourceful Deputy Head at the time, put together a hastily-made plan that will forever linger in the memory of those of us who were there. Not an electronic device in view either. As I wrote to parents:

> We have had a very enjoyable day with those boys who are in school. They have had a morning of different activities – a GK quiz, cookery, hide and seek around the house and snowboard making in DT (which they are about to test in Park). There was plenty of fish and chips to go round at lunch time! After snowy fun outside, they will be heading in for pizza followed by hot chocolate, board games and Christmas party games with the resident staff.

Prep school memories are often created by events that are out of the ordinary, and 'The Day the Wolf Came' was certainly one of the more memorable situations that the school has encountered. An escaped wolf from the Beenham Sanctuary had found its way onto Elstree grounds and was spotted by Olivia roaming on the front lawn by Alec's House as the children were arriving for school. News swept through the school that we had a wolf on the loose and all boys were soon herded into the McMullen Hall to be told that under no circumstances were they to venture outside. Needless to say, this caused plenty of excitement, as well as an element of fear, as the (very gentle) wolf finally made its way off the school site. To my delight, I was approached by a boy in Year 4 who gleefully exclaimed to me after the memorable 'Snow Day':

"This has been my second best ever day at Elstree, Sir!"

"Well, I'm so pleased about that," I replied, "but which day was your best one?"

"Oh, that's easy Sir, it was the day that the wolf came to Elstree."

The past ten years have seen some exciting capital projects come to fruition, most notably the Science Centre, the much-used all-weather Astro named Bates, the development of the Music School, the McMullen Hall, the New Barn conversion at Home Farm and the Reception Classroom extension project in the (now-named) Pre-Prep. It has been a busy time of development during a period of increasing uncertainty for the independent sector.

I am fortunate to have been blessed with two excellent Heads of the Pre-Prep, Kay Markides (Home Farm) and, more recently, Alice Bond, who has almost doubled the pupil numbers in the Pre-Prep in three years, bucking the trend of diminishing pupil numbers in many rural prep schools. I have also had the unstinting support of two outstanding Deputy Heads in Steve Bates and Simon Attwood, whose commitment to Elstree has known no bounds. Tireless workers, meticulous organisers and loyal to the core, they have both played a huge part in the success and happiness of Elstree.

Developments to the curriculum have also kept Elstree at the forefront of prep school education. Whilst holding on to the rigorous and challenging preparation for Common Entrance and Scholarship to the country's leading single-sex and co-educational schools, we continue to offer a broad, progressive and rewarding curriculum, which includes Drama, DT, Art, Music, and Spanish.

Children love adventure and they love opportunity, and we are fortunate to be able to give them the chance to explore their many interests and passions, alongside high academic aspirations. The ability for the boys and girls to choose how to spend their free time and to build up the skills of initiative, resourcefulness and team work gives them a sense of freedom and proper childhood. We want them to appreciate their environment and not to exude any sense of entitlement or swagger.

The hallmark of Elstree has always been its strong sense of family and community, which, in spite of the changes of 175 years, have remained distinctive and special. Olivia and I feel blessed and privileged to be able to lead Elstree with genuine optimism and excitement for the future. The values and qualities that Elstree pupils, staff and parents embrace are timeless. I very much hope our former Headmasters would approve of, and delight at, the Elstree of today; true to the traditions and history of the past 175 years, but remaining relevant and ever-ambitious for a bright and positive future.

As one parent wrote:

> Elstree is an incredibly special school. Looking at senior schools has been quite a challenge, because nowhere else is Elstree.

Pre-Prep fun

Music and Drama

Book Week Parade

Sports Day, 1980s

Sports Day, 2022

Swimming, Tennis, Judo and Fencing

Art and Design & Technology

Cricket, Golf, Cross-country and Hockey

Teaching and Learning – embracing technology

NOTES

Notes for Part One

1 Evelyn Waugh, *Decline and Fall* (Penguin, 1937), p. 14.

2 Donald Leinster-Mackay, *The Rise of the English Prep School* (The Falmer Press, 1984), p. 3.

3 Anthony Glyn, *Kick Turn* (Hutchinson, 1963), p. 98.

4 *Ibid.*

5 *Ibid.*, pp. 96–7.

6 Roger Fry, quoted in Randolph S. Churchill, *Winston S. Churchill, Volume 1 – Youth 1874–1900*, Heinemann, 1966), p. 55.

7 Robin Bell's private memoir, quoted in Vyvyen Brendon, *Prep School Children* (Continuum, 2009), p. 162.

8 Hon. Henry Coke, *Tracks of a Rolling Stone* (Smith, Elder & Co., 1905), p. 9.

9 Édouard Roditi, *Meetings with Conrad* (The Press of the Pegacycle Lady, LA, 1977), pp. 9–10.

10 *Ibid.*, p. 10.

11 Mary E. Richardson, *The Life of a Great Sportsman* (Vinton & Co., 1919), p. 56.

12 L.J. Bernays, *A Manual of Family Prayers and Meditations* (Peacock & Mansfield, 1845), p. 90.

13 Andrew Taylor, *God's Fugitive* (HarperCollins, 1999), p. 10.

14 I.C.M. Sanderson, *A History of Elstree School* (1979), p. 4.

15 *The Times*, 18 October 1937.

16 Lytton Strachey, *Eminent Victorians* (Chatto & Windus, 1918), p. 206.

17 *Dictionary of National Biography*, p. 160.

18 Jonathan Gathorne-Hardy, *The Public School Phenomenon* (Hodder & Stoughton, 1977), p. 83.

19 *Dictionary of National Biography 1912–21*, p. 79.

20 Shane Leslie, *Long Shadows* (John Murray, 1966), p. 22.

21 *Dictionary of National Biography 1931–40*, p. 895.

22 Édouard Roditi, *op. cit.*, p. 12.

23 F.B. Wilson, *Sporting Pie* (Chapman & Hall, 1922), p. 4.

24 Sylvia Townsend Warner, 'A Golden Legend' in *Scenes of Childhood and Other Stories* (Chatto & Windus, 1981), p. 76.

25 Tim Brierly, unpublished note, quoted in Ben Hay, *The Townsend Warners*.

26 Agnes Ridgeway, *Elstree Memories* or *The Lancelot Sandersons in the Eighties* (unpublished memoir, 1941), pp. 9–10 [courtesy of Ben Hay].

27 Agnes Ridgeway, quoted in James Gindin, *John Galsworthy's Life and Art* (The University of Michigan Press, 1987), p. 52.

28 H.V. Marot, *The Life & Letters of John Galsworthy* (Heinemann, 1935), pp. 94–9.

29 M.E. Reynolds, *Memories of John Galsworthy* (Robert Hale, 1936), p. 26.

30 *Ibid.*, p. 27.

31 *Ibid.*

32 Sylvia Townsend Warner, *op. cit.*, p. 79.

33 Dudley Barker, *John Galsworthy, The Man of Principle* (Heinemann, 1963), p. 36.

34 Agnes Ridgeway, *op. cit.*, p. 65.

35 *Ibid.*, p. 202.

36 Michael Cox, *M.R. James* (Oxford University Press, 1983), p. 89.

37 Agnes Ridgeway, *op. cit.*, pp. 73–4.

38 J.W. Lambert, 'The Galsworthy Saga', *Sunday Times*, 9 January 1967.

39 James Gindin, *op. cit.*, p. 62.

40 *Ibid.*, p. 63.

41 E.L. Sanderson notebook, 21 January 1893.

42 *Ibid.*, 26 January 1893 ff.

43 James Gindin, *op. cit.*, p. 64.

44 James Gindin, *op. cit.*, pp. 65–6.

45 Agnes Ridgeway, quoted in James Gindin, *op. cit.*, pp. 166–7.

46 Joseph Conrad, *The Mirror of the Sea* (Methuen, 1906), dedication page.

47 Laurence Davies & J.H. Stape, eds, *Joseph Conrad Letters, Volume 5 – 1920–22* (Cambridge University Press, 1996), p. 583, letter dated May 1916.

48 Laurence Davies & J.H. Stape, eds, *Joseph Conrad Letters, Volume 3 – 1903–07* (Cambridge University Press, 1988), pp. 507–8, letter dated 7 November 1907.

49 Laurence Davies & J.H. Stape, eds, *Joseph Conrad Letters, Volume 7 – 1920–22* (Cambridge University Press, 2007), p. 561, letter dated 30 October 1922.

50 F.B. Wilson, *op. cit.*, p. 4.

51 *The Times*, 1 March 1902.

52 *Dictionary of National Biography, 1941–1950*, p. 560.

53 *The Times*, 20 December 1950.

54 Cecil Headlam, *Walter Headlam – His Letters & Poems* (Duckworth, 1910), p. 16.

55 *Ibid.*, pp. 16–17.

56 Agnes Ridgeway, *op. cit.*, p. 75.

57 Agnes Ridgeway, *op. cit.*, p. 80.

58 *The Edgware Reporter*, 17 December 1887.

59 M.R. James to Mary Emily James, 31 October 1885, quoted in Michael Cox, *M.R. James, An Informal Portrait* (Oxford University Press, 1983), p. 78.

60 Cecil Headlam, *op. cit.*, p. 17.

61 I.C.M. Sanderson, *op. cit.*, p. 15.

62 Jack Churchill to Lady Randolph Churchill, quoted in Celia Lee & John Lee, *The Churchills* (Palgrave Macmillan, 2010), p. 50.

63 Jack Churchill to Lady Randolph Churchill, quoted in Celia Lee & John Lee, *op. cit.*, p. 54.

64 Randolph S. Churchill, *Winston S. Churchill, Companion Volume I, Part 1, 1874–1895* (Houghton Mifflin Company, 1967), p. 232.

65 *The Times*, 16 December 1904.

66 Revd Lancelot Sanderson to Philip Sanderson, 2 September 1901 [courtesy of Ben Hay].

67 *The Times*, 16 December 1904.

68 *The Times*, 22 May 1929.

69 F.B. Wilson, *op. cit.*, pp. 11–12.

70 *The Times*, 28 May 1929.

71 *The Times*, 24 May 1929.

72 F.B. Wilson, *op. cit.*, p. 12.

73 Mildred G. Dooner, *The Last Post: Roll of Officers Who Fell in South Africa 1899–1902* (J.B. Hayward & Son, 1980).

74 *The Times*, 1 May 1929.

75 *The Times*, 29 May 1929.

76 Revd F. de W. Lushington, *Sermons to Young Boys Delivered at Elstree School* (John Murray, 1901), p. v.

77 *Ibid.*, p. vii.

78 *Ibid.*, p. viii.

79 *Ibid.*, p. 8.

80 *Ibid.*, p. 16.

81 *Ibid.*, pp. 102–3.

82 *Ibid.*, p. 8.

83 *The Times*, 12 May 1952.

84 *The Times*, 22 January 1965.

85 Agnes Sanderson, quoted in Catherine Dupré, *John Galsworthy, A Biography* (Collins, 1976), p. 40.

86 Laurence Davies & J.H. Stape, eds, *Joseph Conrad Letters, Volume 4 – 1908–11* (Cambridge University Press, 1990), p. 388, letter dated 30 October 1922.

87 A.J. Richardson to Lady Gregory, from 'My Grief', in *Seventy Years*, quoted in *Robert Gregory 1881–1918* (Colin Smythe, 1981), p. 26.

88 George Bernard Shaw to Lady Gregory, 5 February 1918, quoted in Michael Holroyd, *Bernard Shaw – The Pursuit of Power (Volume II)* (Chatto & Windus, 1989), p. 393.

89 Sebastian Faulks, *Birdsong* (Vintage, 2004), p. 4.

90 Édouard Roditi, *op. cit.*, pp. 6–7.

91 *Ibid.*

92 *Ibid.*, *passim.*

93 Charles Riley to author, 25 July 2022.

94 *Salvo*, 19 July 1971.

95 Sandy Wilson, *I Could Be Happy* (Michael Joseph, 1975), p. 34.

96 *Ibid.*

97 *Ibid.*, pp. 34–5.

98 *Ibid.*, p. 35.

99 *Ibid.*

100 *Ibid.*

101 *Ibid.*, p. 36.

102 Sir Alistair Horne, 'Introduction', in Michael Tillotson, *Dwin Bramall* (Sutton Publishing, 2005), p. v.

103 The late Lord Bramall interview with author, 20 March 2015.

104 Michael Tillotson, *op. cit.*, p. 8.

105 *Ibid.*; & interview with author, 20 March 2015.

106 Christopher Blount to author, 26 March 2015.

107 Robert Stainton, 'Life at Old Elstree', quoted in Richard Russell, *Elstree School Woolhampton 1939–1989*, p. 2.
108 *The Times*, 28 March 1939.
109 Laurence Davies & J.H. Stape, eds, *Joseph Conrad Letters, Volume 7*, pp. 507–8, letter dated 7 November 1907.

110 Robert Stainton, *op. cit.*, p. 2.
111 *Ibid.*, pp. 2–3.
112 Richard Hanbury-Tenison to Terrence McMullen, 30 April 2000.
113 Richard Hanbury-Tenison diary, 30 April 2000.

Notes for Part Two

1 *Salvo 1997/98*, p. 34.
2 *Ibid.*
3 Messrs Beadel, Wood & Co sale document, 9 July 1907.
4 Terrence McMullen tribute, *Salvo Lent/Summer Terms 1979*, p. 5.
5 Sebastian Faulks, Elstree manuscript, seen 23 April 2018.
6 Confidential note from Commander Ian Sanderson, found in the attics at Elstree.
7 Derived from miscellaneous notes by Commander Ian Sanderson, found in the attics at Elstree.
8 Ian Sanderson to Geoffrey Fisher, Archbishop of Canterbury, 1947 (Elstree Archives).
9 *The Times*, 11 June 1942.
10 *The Times*, 11 August 1942.
11 Clipping from a local paper, November 1943, preserved in Ian Sanderson's album.
12 *The Times*, 19 May 1941.
13 Ben Hay to author, 7 October 2022.
14 *Ibid.*
15 *Ibid.*
16 Peter Vereker to Terrence McMullen, 28 April 2000.
17 Peter Vereker obituary, *Daily Telegraph*, 20 November 2001.
18 Peter Vereker to Terrence McMullen, 28 April 2000.
19 Ian Sanderson to Revd R.J.B. Eddison, 10 July 1950.
20 Revd R.J.B. Eddison to David Cooper, 11 July 1950.
21 David Cooper to author, 2011.
22 Tim Christie to author, 12 October 2022.
23 Andrew Birkin to Terrence McMullen, 30 April 2000.

24 Andrew Birkin to author, 11 January 2023.
25 Ian Sanderson to the parents, 1 December 1958.
26 Lord Fellowes to author, 10 January 2018
27 *Ibid.*
28 Tim Christie to author, 12 October 2022.
29 Debs McMullen to author, 16 January 2023.
30 Charles Riley to author, 25 July 2022.
31 'Elstree Notes', *Salvo Lent/Summer Terms 1987*, p. 2.
32 Nigel Saxby-Soffe to the school, 13 August 2018.
33 Ian Sanderson to the parents, 29 July 1958.
34 Ben Hay to author, 7 October 2022.
35 Terrence McMullen headmaster speech, quoted in *Salvo Lent Term 1984*, p. 34.
36 Confidential note from Commander Ian Sanderson, found in the attics at Elstree.
37 Ian Sanderson to P.R. Faulks, 14 May 1961 (Elstree Archives).
38 Sebastian Faulks, Elstree manuscript, seen 23 April 2018.
39 *Ibid.*
40 *Ibid.*
41 *Ibid.*
42 Charles Fox to author, 6 November 2022.
43 Ian Sanderson to the parents, 20 December 1960.
44 *The Times*, 7 September 2004.
45 Revd John Eddison, 'Prologue' in I.C.M. Sanderson, *A History of Elstree School and Three Generations of the Sanderson Family* (privately printed, 1979), p. vii.
46 *The Times*, 16 September 2004.
47 Debs McMullen (Burles) to author, 17 January 2023.
48 *The Times*, 11 June 1974.

49 Terrence McMullen to David Cooper, 20 June 1974.
50 David Cooper sports day speech, 22 June 1974.
51 Michael Coates, McMullen memorial address, St Mary's Church, Funtington, 19 August 2004.
52 *The Pink*, 15 December 1988.
53 Humphrey Southern to Terrence McMullen, *c.* 2000.
54 George Monbiot, *The Guardian*, 7 November 2019.
55 *Salvo*, July 1972.
56 John Henderson to Terrence McMullen, 14 November 1990.
57 Francis Long to Terrence McMullen, 9 May 2000.
58 Hereward Swallow to Terrence McMullen, 7 May 2000.
59 Charles Riley to author, 25 July 2022.
60 *Ibid.*
61 Rachel Antelme (McMullen) to Terrence McMullen, 11 August 2000.
62 Brian Hewitt address, quoted in *Salvo Lent/Summer Term 1979*, p.6.
63 Terrence McMullen, *A Short Guide to Good Conduct* (1979; revised 1982), *passim*.
64 *Ibid.*
65 Steve Bates to author, 26 November 2022.
66 *Ibid.*
67 Terrence McMullen to Alick Hay, 5 August 1982.
68 Richard Russell, *Vermilion, Sage and Ecru* (privately printed, 2007), p. 118.
69 *The Pink*, 24 September 1987.
70 *The Pink*, 14 October 1993.
71 *Salvo Autumn 1983*, p. 13.
72 *Salvo Autumn 1985*, p. 8.
73 *Salvo Lent/Summer 1987*, p.13.
74 *Salvo Lent/Summer 1984*, p. 20.
75 *Ibid.*, p. 19.
76 *The Pink*, 6 July 1990.
77 *Ibid.*
78 Terrence McMullen to David Cooper, 1 December 1992.
79 *Salvo Summer 1999* (note by Micky Watson, July 1999), p. 57.
80 *Salvo 1994/95*, p. 3.
81 Syd Hill to author, 31 December 2022.
82 Syd Hill farewell speech, July 2008, quoted in *Salvo Summer 2008*, p. 70.
83 Syd Hill to author, 13 August 2017.
84 Headmaster's speech, 8 June 1996, quoted in *Salvo 1995/96*, p. 23.
85 Jane Hill to Terrence McMullen, 2004.
86 Prue Matchwick to author, 28 November 2022.
87 Simon Atwood to author, 26 November 2022.
88 *Salvo 1999/2000*, p. 19.
89 *Ibid.*
90 *Salvo 2000/2001*, p. 8.
91 *Salvo 1999/2000*, p. 35.
92 Syd Hill speech, 23 June 2001, quoted in *Salvo 2000/2001*, pp. 37–8.
93 *Ibid.*, p. 50.
94 Syd Hill speech, 21 June 2003, quoted in *Salvo 2002/2003*, pp. 54–5.
95 ISC/ISI Inspection report, 13–17 October 2003.
96 *Independent Schools Inspection Report*, November 2009, p. 7.
97 *Salvo Summer 2008*, p. 4.
98 Steve Bates to author, 26 November 2022.
99 Syd Hill Farewell speech, July 2008, quoted in *Salvo Summer 2008*, p. 68.
100 *Tatler Schools Guide*, 2011.
101 *Salvo 2013*, p. 109.
102 *Salvo 2016*, p. 118.
103 *Salvo 2013*, p. 107.
104 Olivia Inglis to author, 26 November 2022.
105 Sid Inglis to author, 8 July 2022.
106 Olivia Inglis to author, 26 November 2022.
107 *Ibid.*
108 Sid Inglis to parents, 22 May 2014.
109 *Salvo 2014*, p. 102.
110 Sid Inglis to parents, 18 October 2019.
111 Sid Inglis to parents, 4 September 2018.
112 Olivia Inglis to author, 26 November 2022.
113 Olivia Inglis to author, 26 November 2022.
114 Crispy Kidson comment, *Echo 18*, January 2021, p. 4.
115 Steve Bates to author, 26 November 2022.
116 Sid Inglis to author, 8 July 2022.
117 Olivia Inglis to author, 26 November 2022.
118 Sid Inglis to author, 22 September 2022.
119 *Salvo 2019*, p. 133.
120 Speech by A.C. Parsons, Chairman of the Governors, July 1976.

INDEX

THE AUTHOR

Hugo Vickers is well known as a biographer, lecturer and broadcaster, and is an acknowledged expert on the Royal Family. He is called upon to commentate on important state occasions, and at times when the Royal Family are in the news. He has covered events from the first wedding of the Prince of Wales, the funerals of Diana, the Queen Mother, Prince Philip, and Queen Elizabeth II and most recently the Coronation of King Charles III. In 2018 the *Financial Times* described him as: 'the most knowledgeable royal biographer on the planet.'

He is a Deputy Lieutenant for the Royal County of Berkshire and Captain of the Lay Stewards of St George's Chapel, Windsor Castle. He lives in London and Wiltshire and has three grown-up children, two of whom are Old Boys of Elstree.